A HARVEST OF
FAITHFULNESS

A HARVEST OF
FAITHFULNESS

Tools to Cultivate the Fruit of the Spirit

REBEKAH MONTGOMERY

PROMISE
PRESS
An Imprint of Barbour Publishing

Published by Promise Press, an imprint of Barbour Publishing, Inc., P.O. Box 719, Uhrichsville, Ohio 44683 http://www.barbourbooks.com

 Member of the
Evangelical Christian
Publishers Association

Printed in the United States of America.

Dedication

To John, my faithful husband

Chapter 1

The Meaning of Faith and Faithfulness

Faith in God coupled with our faithfulness to God are the legs that support our walk with Him. The more we trust God to be faithful to us, the more we will be willing to step out to do His will and the farther and faster we will move forward His kingdom on earth.

Now faith is being sure of what we hope for and certain of what we do not see.

HEBREWS 11:1 NIV

I held them in my hand, taking care not to even breathe on them. Any stray wind zephyr would have broadcast the very tiny seeds far and wide.

I had harvested them myself, shaking them out of a plant that was almost a tree.

It wasn't the first mustard plant I had ever seen, but it was certainly the largest. I was very familiar with the shoulder-high wild mustard plants that grew along the ditches of the Midwest. But because frost comes before they can achieve full height, those little sprouts looked Lilliputian compared with this Middle Eastern giant!

I had often puzzled what Jesus meant when He said that the kingdom of God was like a mustard seed, until I saw the plants He was referring to in their full glory. They were, indeed, the greatest of the herbs!

The mustard seed—how infinitesimal! But by divine design, upon germination, it can achieve the proportions of an impressive tree. Birds roost on and feed from its branches. The spicy yellow flowers and leaves provide pleasant shade for the weary wayfarer.

It really doesn't take much to make a difference for the kingdom—just the small seeds of faith and faithfulness planted in Jesus to produce roots and branches that stretch far into the everlasting. Moment by moment, day by day, faithfully plant mustard seeds and reap an eternal harvest.

Faithfully plant mustard seeds of love by caring for each and every person—even if it is only a little bit.

Faithfully plant mustard seeds of joy by sharing a delight.

Faithfully plant mustard seeds of peace by turning the other cheek.

Faithfully plant mustard seeds of patience by letting someone go ahead of you.

Faithfully plant mustard seeds of kindness with thoughtful gestures.

Faithfully plant mustard seeds of goodness by meeting a need.

Faithfully plant mustard seeds of gentleness by soothing a hurt.

Faithfully plant mustard seeds of self-control by controlling your impulses.

Based on MATTHEW 13, GALATIANS 5:22–23

*Faith is
two empty hands
held open to receive
all of the Lord Jesus.*

ALAN REDPATH

What is Faith?

As Christians, we talk a lot about faith. But do we really know what we mean when we use this word? Do we mean simply our religion? Or do we mean a happy, hopeful feeling of optimism? Is faith something we can work hard to produce in our lives? Or is faith a heart attitude, a willingness to say "Yes" to God no matter what? When that occurs, faith has becomes faithfulness.

The Scripture's Definition of Faith:

> *Now faith is*
> *the substance of things hoped for,*
> *the evidence of things not seen.*
> HEBREWS 11:1

Webster's Definition:
1. belief, trust, and loyalty to God; 2. firm belief in something for which there is no proof; 3. complete trust

The Scripture's Definition of Faithfulness:

> *Let us throw off everything that hinders*
> *and the sin that so easily entangles,*
> *and let us run with perseverance the race*
> *that is marked out for us.*
> HEBREWS 12:1 NIV

A HARVEST OF FAITHFULNESS

Webster's Definition:
    1. loyal; 2. conscientious; 3. reliable

An Acronym for Faith:
Fully
Anticipating
It
To
Happen

An Acronym for Faithful:
Following
Always
In
True–
Hearted
Fellowship and
Unity with the
Lord

Faith is more than words;

it is action. . .

it is cooperating with the promises

and power of God.

Tim Roehl
Surprised by Grace

"Will you still love me," she asked, her entrancing almond-shaped eyes regarding him tentatively, "if I tell you that I've been unfaithful and probably will be unfaithful again?"

He knew that what she said was true. She was the town prostitute. Every man in the village had known her. Every male newcomer would.

"It does not nor will it change my love for you," he told her earnestly, honestly.

"Perhaps it would be better if I cleaned up a little before we married," she said. "Stopped. . ." He laid his finger on her lips so she would say no more. He knew well what she did, that she prostituted herself, but it pained him to hear her recite her flaws. He saw her youth and foolishness; he knew the awful forces that drove her to the depths to which she had fallen. He knew, too, that she couldn't extricate herself from the quagmire without help. His love made it his privilege to extend it.

"Hush," he told her. "From this moment on, that is all in the past. I will never mention it to you again. There is only the future."

But Hosea's heart was apprehensive. He had long loved Gomer, but he could only dream of the day that she would return his affections. She was only marrying him now because he was convenient and she was in some sort of trouble. He thought she might even be pregnant.

Gomer—whose very name meant corruption—was the daughter of Diblaim, a famous harlot. Any pastor, parent, or marriage counselor in the world would have told him that he was a fool for marrying such a girl, but in this most unusual case, God had spoken clearly to the young prophet.

"Marry a woman who is an adulteress and claim the children of her unfaithfulness as your own," the Almighty had said. Hosea's faithful love for his licentious wife was to serve as a living illustration of God's steadfast, yearning love to His wayward people.

In the same tender way that God accepts us as we are, Hosea took Gomer to his bosom well aware of her past and reputation. And hoped.

When the first child, a boy, was born, Hosea anxiously examined him for any resemblance, however slight, to himself. Could he be his own flesh? Hosea swallowed hard. The baby was his beloved's child, so he became Hosea's own.

By the time the next two children were born, she was so blasé about her infidelities, there was little doubt that the children were not Hosea's. She was so secure in Hosea's unflinching love for her that she rubbed his nose in her unfaithfulness. He pleaded with her to stop. He begged her, but she was shopping for a better deal. Love was one thing; money was another.

Then she thought she found the step up. The man so bedecked her with jewelry and baubles, turned her head so completely that she even forgot Hosea and the children existed. They would see her pass on the street leaning on his arm, suggestively dressed, her eyes painted, her hair elaborately arranged. Soon it was a different man. Then another. Then another. A whole sordid string of them. Then the family heard the awful news. She had lost everything—and more. She was to be sold as a slave to repay her debts.

Hosea hoped she would send word to him and beg him for his help. He waited. Nothing. Then he heard there was another man involved who also loved her. Maybe he should just stay out of the picture.

Then the word of God came to Hosea. "Go show your love again to your wife. She is an adulteress and she's loved by another man, but go love her as I have loved Israel even though they chase after other gods."

"Who will buy this woman?" the slave seller asked a bored crowd. He tore Gomer's dress to reveal her body and hopefully stir a little interest. In her nakedness, she looked used up, tired, and old. Her lover offered a single shekel. No one bid up the price.

"This is not enough for such a woman!" shouted the seller. He jerked her around and slapped her bare shoulders. "See! She's strong yet and healthy! A good field hand!"

Another shekel was added. Her lover made it three.

It was slow going. Every man had already possessed her, sampled her, used her. Why buy her? She could be had for free. Tediously, the price rose. Six shekels. Ten shekels. Then it stopped. Her lover had the bid for ten shekels.

"Fifteen shekels," said Hosea.

"Sold!" cried the seller.

She turned and saw her husband. And began to shake. Here before her stood the man who had loved her, made her his wife, gave her his protection, and wholly accepted her children. Here was the man whom she had betrayed, exploited, and despised but who now held the power of life over her in his hand. He owned her. He could do anything he wanted with her. He could exact whatever vengeance he desired.

And Hosea said to her what God says to every prodigal whom He purchased with the lifeblood of His Son, "Come home to me. You will be my beloved."

Based on the Book of HOSEA

One Day in Heaven

In a dream I found myself in a palace in another world. The air itself tingled around me. I could sense, smell, hear, and see things I had never before detected.

In this beautiful palace—one that was beyond any words to describe—I gaped in awe at the bright beings who milled about me. When they noticed me, they drew back from me with expressions of horror, and to my shame, I realized I was dressed in stained, dirty rags, and my skin was caked with filth. I thought that perhaps I had better leave. But as I was hunting for the door, a great hush fell as the Lord God Himself entered the room and seated Himself upon the throne. Spontaneously, the bright beings bowed themselves before Him, casting all of their possessions at His feet. For a time, I was aware of only Him. His brightness. His beauty. Then, with creeping dread, I became conscious of His awesome holiness. In the bright light that emanated from His presence, I saw myself without any illusions. My clothing was not merely stained—it was foul. My skin was not merely dirty—it was fetid. Desperate to escape His presence, I tried to hide.

Then, to my horror, one of the bright beings pointed directly at me. "What is that doing in Your presence, Lord?"

All of the bright beings shrank away from me. But then Someone else came toward me. This Person put His arm around me and held me close. "It's okay, Father," He told the Almighty. "This one's with Me." Then, before my very eyes, my ragged, dirty clothing was transformed into a spotless white robe. My skin shone like the sun. I stared at my now-clean hands in disbelief until the Person held out His nail-scarred one, and I placed my hand in His. Around me, the bright beings began to sing and clap with joy. The One on the throne reached down to me. "Come here, My child." He picked me up and sat me on His lap. His heart throbbed in my ear. "Now," He said, "tell me everything."

Faith is God's gift to us, a sign of His love and grace. It grows out of our intimate, loving relationship with the Father, made possible by Christ's redemption. Faithfulness is our sign to Him of our commitment to the relationship.

*For ye are
all the children of God
by faith in Christ Jesus.*

GALATIANS 3:26

*When life comes rushing at us,
threatening to destroy us,
our faith in God is what holds us stable.*

*Faith is
the soul riding at anchor.*

JOSH BILLINGS

Abraham closed his eyes and hid himself in the darkness of faith, and therein he found light eternal.

- Faith is a free surrender and a joyous wager on the unseen, untried, and unknown goodness of God. . . . To have faith is to have God.

- Faith unites the soul with the invisible, ineffable, unutterable, eternal, unthinkable word of God, while at the same time it separates it from all things visible and tangible.

- It is a living fountain springing up into life everlasting.

MARTIN LUTHER

Spiritual Eyes

*Faith is believing beyond
the messages of the optic nerve.*
ANONYMOUS

Faith is like radar
which sees through the fog—
the reality of things at a distance
that the human eye cannot see.

CORRIE TEN BOOM

By faith a man moves through darkness;
but he moves securely, his hand in the hand of God.
He is literally seeing through the eyes of God.
WALTER FARRELL

Faith is the capacity to
perceive the abiding. . .
in the transitory,
the invisible in the visible.

LEO BAECK

When I was a young girl, I wanted a pony. I read about ponies, dreamed about ponies, pretended the broom was a pony, and prayed that God would send me one. I prayed so fervently that some mornings I'd race to the window and look out at the pasture beside the barn, expecting to see a pony knee-deep in the Queen Anne's lace, country breezes blowing through its silky mane and tail.

I began saving my money in a mason jar under my bed to buy a pony. I put my allowance in there, with a prayer that God would send me a pony. When I was saving so desperately, it hurt sometimes to give a tithe to God, but I went ahead and gave Him 10 percent of all my nickels. I knew it would take about $50 to buy a pony, and at a quarter a week for my allowance, I expected to buy my small horse shortly before my thirtieth birthday. I knew I needed a miracle, but I was counting on God to supply one. I figured the money would be for equestrian incidentals when the pony arrived.

Then the missionaries came to our church. They showed their overexposed slides of little children from across the ocean hearing the gospel for the first time. Some of the children walked to the mission school and churches from far away. Some had no parents but were cared for by missionaries. Although mostly what I saw were dark smudges with blinding white teeth, I was very moved.

The missionary asked us to pray for the children, then passed the offering plate. As I bowed my head to pray, I "saw" my mason jar under my bed.

Then came a mighty internal struggle. Did God want me to give away that money? Should I put it in the plate to help people I would never meet this side of Heaven? Surely God would understand if I saved it for my pony.

I slept little that night. Toward morning, I dragged my jar out, opened the zinc lid, and poured on my bed the coins that had been so painstakingly saved. Five dollars and twenty cents. Chores, birthday money, allowance, pennies rescued from the gutter—all saved a cent at a time.

"It's Yours, Lord," I told Him.

That night at the mission conference, I opened my mason jar and poured the change in the offering plate. A penny bounced over the rim, hit the floor on its edge, and rolled down to the altar, as if it were anxious to present itself to the Lord. I watched it go with tears in my eyes.

From that point, I let go of my pony dreams. I saved my money halfheartedly, buying penny candy occasionally, a package of Barbie shoes, or a folder of paper dolls. I wondered about the little children in Africa and hoped to introduce myself when I got to Heaven. Maybe I would find a pony in the Queen Anne's lace outside my heavenly mansion.

Then my mother took me to visit my uncle. He lived about 350 miles away from us on a wild farm with herds of shaggy, unkempt stock, including horses and ponies. Gazing over the fence at his ponies, I tried to make adult conversation with him.

"How much does a pony cost these days?" I asked.

Offhandedly, he remarked, "If you want a pony, I'll give you one."

I was thunderstruck and a little doubtful. Was this just one of those things that adults said to children? Would he remember?

Within a week of us returning home, a check arrived in the mail. Within a month, a pony was standing in the pasture next to the barn, knee-deep in Queen Anne's lace, the country breezes ruffling through its silky mane and tail. I was grateful to my uncle. But I knew whom I really had to thank. My silent prayer of thanksgiving winged heavenward.

For me, faith was the substance of ponies hoped for and a lesson that God rewards the walk of faithfulness with a ride of joy!

Spiritual Feet

Faith is the foot of the soul by which it can march along the road of the commandments. Love can make the feet move more swiftly, but faith is the foot that carries the soul. Faith is the oil enabling the wheels of holy devotion and of earnest piety to move well; and without faith the wheels are taken from the chariot, and we drag heavily. With faith I can do all things; without faith I shall neither have the inclination nor the power to do anything in the service of God. . . . Would you be comfortable and happy? Would you enjoy religion? Would you have the religion of cheerfulness and not that of gloom? Then "have faith in God" (Mark 11:22). If you love darkness and are satisfied to dwell in gloom and misery, then be content with little faith; but if you love sunshine and would sing songs of rejoicing, covet earnestly this best gift—"great faith." CHARLES H. SPURGEON

For we walk by faith, not by sight.

2 CORINTHIANS 5:7

How Beautiful Are the Feet

To many people, it was a strange ritual, one that made them snicker behind their hands. "They wash feet," they would whisper about the neighboring congregation, their noses wrinkled in disgust.

Even within the church itself, some members wanted to abandon the practice. They just didn't want to do it anymore. They didn't like other congregations and denominations looking down on them, and the act itself was humiliating and degrading, they said. This was the 1960s, after all, a time when human dignity was to be recognized.

While the controversy over foot washing swirled at denominational headquarters and little whirlwinds of it eddied through the small rural congregations, one particular congregation still planned to do it. On Good Friday, they would wash feet and partake of Communion. There wasn't a gun to anybody's head. Nobody had to participate who didn't want to.

On that night, the church was still. Even the pianist had the night off. Outside, a chilly shower rattled against the stained-glass window. For this service only, men and boys sat on one side of the church, women and girls on the other. They sat in quiet reflection, searching their hearts. Did they have sin they had failed to confess? Had they wronged someone? Were they holding a secret grudge? These issues must be brought before the judgment seat within the private chambers of each heart. If crimes had been committed and the guilt unresolved, then they would not take Communion until restitution was made.

The pastor rose to his feet and faced the congregation, Bible in hand, and read: "Now before the feast of the passover, when Jesus knew that his hour was come that he should depart out of this world unto the Father, having loved his own which were in the world, he loved them unto the end" (John 13:1).

He read aloud the story of how Jesus gird Himself with a towel and washed the feet of His disciples. Peter objected, "Lord, doest thou wash my feet?" and Jesus assured him, "If I wash thee not, thou hast no part with me." "Wash all of me," begged Peter. "It's not necessary," Jesus told him, and all in the congregation understood Peter's enthusiasm. He wanted to be part of Jesus. He wanted to be clean of the guilt he carried.

Without commentary, the women and girls adjourned to one room and the men and boys to a separate one. They removed their shoes and socks, and sat in self-conscious circles. One after another, they knelt next to their neighbors and washed their feet.

Tears began to flow as one humbly knelt before another, took the feet and gently splashed water over them into the basin, then lovingly scooped the water over the instep with cupped hands. Toes were dried one at a time, with the same attention a mother shows tiny baby feet. Seeing friends, neighbors, kinfolk on their knees performing such a menial task—knowing that the Creator of the universe did the same and continues to do so each time we sin—is almost too much to bear.

Without warning, a mother-in-law said to her daughter-in-law, "Forgive me!" Father said to son, "I'm sorry!" Neighbor to neighbor, "There was no excuse for what I did to you!" As they saw Jesus in the person of their neighbor, each found the courage to confess sin, seek forgiveness, and find peace.

This is true faithfulness—to imitate Jesus by being the servant of all.

Faithful Servants

"The kingdom of heaven. . .will be like a man going on a journey, who called his servants and entrusted his property to them. . . . After a long time the master of those servants returned and settled accounts with them. . . . His master replied, 'Well done, good and faithful servant! You have been faithful with a few things; I will put you in charge of many things. Come and share your master's happiness!' "

MATTHEW 25:1, 14, 19, 21 NIV

God wants people whom He can depend upon. . . . God can be depended upon. He wants us to be just as decided, just as reliable, just as stable. This is what faith means. God is looking for men on whom He can put the weight of all His life and power and faithful promises. When God finds such a soul there is nothing He will not do for him.

A. B. SIMPSON

Living a life of faith means never knowing where you are being led. But it does mean loving and knowing the One who is leading. It is literally a life of faith, not of understanding and reason—a life of knowing Him who calls us to go. Faith is rooted in the knowledge of a Person. . . .

OSWALD CHAMBERS

In the broad world of man's total voyage through time to eternity, faith is not only a gracious companion, but an essential guide.

THEODORE M. HESBURG

A HARVEST OF FAITHFULNESS

I learned a lot about faithful friendship from a mutt.

Many years ago, I sat on the wooden steps of my country parsonage home and moodily regarded the dried-up cornfield beyond the rail fence just east of the house. The cornstalks were dead; their bones stripped clean, their spines snapped by the corn picker. Tassel tops like skeleton hands on bony arms waved feebly from the frozen, snow-covered ground.

It had been an awful day at school, and I didn't want to go back—ever. It started with my clothes: Mom had made me wear leggings. They were scratchy as steel wool, UGLY, UGLY, UGLY; and I was too old to wear them.

I had had a bout with pneumonia the previous year, and Mom thought my health was more important than fashion. I strongly disagreed. I thought she had totally forgotten what it was like to be in sixth grade, trapped in a body that didn't know whether it was a girl's or a woman's. Today, it was a woman's and too old to wear leggings—especially ugly ones that got me teased both coming and going to school by a boy on the bus. Nor had they escaped the scornful critique of the cloakroom fashion experts. My face still burned with shame.

Yo-yo, our black dog, a cocker spaniel-hound-mutt, came and sat beside me, her stubby fringed tail beating a friendly staccato on the peeling porch step. She was pretty old, the veteran of a lot of romps through the woods, swims in the neighbor's pond, puppies, tick and flea infestations, and camp outs. But she was a real trouper at doll buggy rides and tea parties. Invited cat guests regularly ran off—often wearing our best doll clothes—but not Yo-yo; she stuck it out, just happy to be included and to be our companion.

Now she listened as I poured out my humiliation at having to wear leggings; Mother's indifference to style; the boy's cruelty on the bus; the snotty, bare-legged girls at school. . .the unfathomable cosmic unfairness of it all! Where was God when Mother made me wear those horrible things? Why hadn't He struck that boy mute as he uttered his first jeer? Or better yet, smitten all of those tittering girls with a horrible plague? Why had I been born to endure such suffering? If God were a God of love, why had He allowed all of this?

If Yo-yo knew the answers to these unanswerable questions, she held her peace. She did offer one very practical antidote to the bitterness of life: Her brown eyes liquid with sympathetic love, she licked my ear.

How often since that day, when mired down in a muddy pothole on the straight and narrow path to Life, have I been the recipient of similar faithful love from fellow Christian believers! No, they didn't lick my ear—but they did let me know they cared. They had the patience and restraint to let me talk it out—regardless of the depth of my ignorance and stupidity or the length of time required before I made sense. Then, when I was ready to hear, they gave me an encouraging word, a helpful

Scripture, a personal experience, and sometimes, a healing rebuke that incised the infectious sores festering in my soul.

Like Yo-yo, they demonstrated God's faithfulness to me, a model for me to use as my own life's pattern.

There are two ways of believing. First, to believe that there is a God. This kind of faith is knowledge, or information, rather than faith as such. Secondly, there is faith in God. This faith I possess when I not only hold that what is said about God is true, but when I put my whole trust in Him, undertake to deal with Him personally, and believe without doubt that I shall find Him to be and to do as I have been told. MARTIN LUTHER

Faith is an awareness of divine. . . companionship, a form of communion between God and man.

ABRAHAM JOSHUA HESCHEL

A HARVEST OF FAITHFULNESS

Faith furnishes
prayer with wings,
without which it cannot
soar to Heaven.

JOHN CLIMACUS

The desire for certitude is natural enough and explains the human tendency to mistake faith for certainty. This is not a specially religious mistake. We think of supernaturalism when faith is mentioned, but the naturalistic description of the world also operates on assumptions that require a faith as robust as does the most soaring mysticism. The usual efforts to skirt faith beg all the questions there are. A psychiatrist, for instance, who points out to you that you believe in God the Father because you need a father, or that you became a missionary to expiate your guilt feelings, may be quite correct, but he has not touched on the prior question as to whether there is, in fact, a cosmic father figure who is the archetype of all other fathers, or whether there is an evangel worth spending your life promulgating.
THOMAS HOWARD
Christ the Tiger

Faith means being grasped by a power that is greater than we are, a power that shakes us and turns us, and transforms and heals us. Surrender to this power of faith.

PAUL TILLICH

God our Father has made all things depend on faith so that whoever has faith will have everything, and whoever does not have faith will have nothing.

MARTIN LUTHER

Faith is

the soul's consciousness

of its divine relationship

and exalted destiny.

G. S. MERRIAM

A HARVEST OF FAITHFULNESS

Faith is response to love's dear call,
Of love's dear face the sight;
To do love's bidding now is all
That gives the heart delight.
To love thy voice and to reply,
"Lord, here am I."

As blows the wind through summer trees,
And all the leaves are stirred,
O Spirit, move as thou dost please,
My heart yields at thy word.
Faith hears thee calling from beyond
And doth respond.

"What thou dost will—that I desire,
Through me let it be done,
Thy will and mine in love's own fire
Are welded into one."
"Lord, I believe!" Nay, rather say,
"Lord, I obey."

HANNAH HURNARD

In a marriage, we commit ourselves to one another because of love. But our faithfulness is lived out daily, even on the days when we don't feel particularly loving.

In our Christian life, we commit ourselves to God because of love. But our faithfulness to Him means an ongoing, daily obedience, even when we feel afraid or sad or full of doubts.

Nothing in life is more wonderful than faith— the one great moving force which we can neither weigh in the balance nor test in the crucible.

SIR WILLIAM OSLER

Many of us are faithful to our ideas about Jesus Christ, but how many of us are faithful to Jesus Himself? Faithfulness to Jesus means that I must step out even when and where I can't see any-thing (see Matthew 14:29). But faithfulness to my own ideas means that I first clear the way mentally. Faith, however, is not intellectual understanding; faith is a deliberate commitment to the Person of Jesus Christ, even when I can't see the way ahead. OSWALD CHAMBERS

Faith is a living, bold confidence in the grace of God.

MARTIN LUTHER

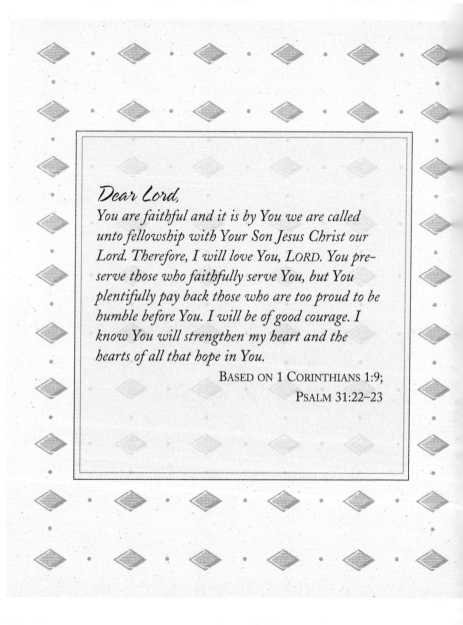

Dear Lord,
You are faithful and it is by You we are called
unto fellowship with Your Son Jesus Christ our
Lord. Therefore, I will love You, LORD. You pre-
serve those who faithfully serve You, but You
plentifully pay back those who are too proud to be
humble before You. I will be of good courage. I
know You will strengthen my heart and the
hearts of all that hope in You.

BASED ON 1 CORINTHIANS 1:9;
PSALM 31:22–23

Chapter 2

Planting the Seeds of Faithfulness

"If ye have faith as a grain of mustard seed,
ye shall say unto this mountain,
Remove hence to yonder place;
and it shall remove;
and nothing shall be impossible unto you."
MATTHEW 17:20

For by grace are ye saved
through faith;
and that not of yourselves:
it is the gift of God.
EPHESIANS 2:8

Fruitful Seeds of Faithfulness
Planted by the Master Gardener

True faithfulness—the Galatians 5 genus, which is the fruit of the Spirit—goes beyond the usual garden variety of human faithfulness that we regularly encounter. True faithfulness reaches back to the Garden of Eden and reintroduces us to Person-to-person faithfulness at its most pristine.

Here God the Father Himself planted the first seeds of faithfulness for His newly formed offspring by providing for their every need, their every wish—pests in the Garden notwithstanding. Faith is not something we can earn; it is not something we can work hard to achieve. Instead, it is a gift from God. His grace plants the seeds of faith in our hearts, where they wait for the nourishing rain of the Spirit.

Christ's Life
The Fragrant Blooms That Yield
the Seeds of Faithfulness in Our Hearts

A very human but totally divine faithfulness burst into rare bloom in the Garden of Gethsemane when Jesus prayed and sweat blood while His disciples slept off their heavy meal. It was His life's darkest hour, and He had every provocation to call down fire from Heaven to consume His callous disciples—or at least properly frighten them into staying awake with Him.

Instead, His faithful heart prayed for them—and us. Our faith is the result of His prayers. The faith of others may be a result of your prayers.

I thought on my ways,

and turned my feet

unto thy testimonies.

I made haste,

and delayed not to keep

thy commandments.

PSALM 119:59–60

In Ghana, West Africa, it is called a "Gethsemane Night."

Planned for the Thursday before Good Friday, the interiors of churches are swathed with branches and bedecked with flowers to resemble a garden. But the worshippers do not gather to enjoy the greenery, but to commemorate the actions of Jesus in the garden when He sweat as if it were great drops of blood, prayed for the world, and finally submitted to the Father's will of death on the cross.

In addition to remembering, they seek to fulfill the request that Jesus made of His disciples to watch with Him and pray lest they fall into temptation.

To seek God's fortification against temptation is to admit that we are bunglers with weaknesses that have the potential of destroying our lives and keeping us from faithfully fulfilling God's purpose for us. The disciples clearly showed their weakness: They slept, satiated by a big meal, their flesh satisfied, while Jesus agonized. What Jesus asked of them was not as important to them as a short nap.

Jesus felt it was so vital that we pray about our potential for sin that He included it in the prayer He taught His disciples: "Lead us not into temptation, but deliver us from the evil one" (Matthew 6:13 NIV).

In order to be faithful, we must take clear stock of our weaknesses. To recognize where Satan may attack prepares us to accept God's victory over our weaknesses. It enables us to be continually faithful to God's purpose.

I Heard Him Through the Grapevine

Once upon a time, while living on our little farm in Ohio, my husband and I found a dried-up grapevine among the department store markdowns at the end of the planting season. It was an unpromising bit of vegetation, but we bought it anyway. I had idyllic childhood memories of lying under the neighbor's shady grape arbor on hot August days. I also remembered playing war with the ripening fruit. (The grapes were purple, and we could always tell who was "wounded" by the purple stains splattered across their arms and faces.) I thought of sucking the luscious fruit out of the skin and later eating jelly on homemade bread; I wanted my children to have some of those same experiences. So my husband and I dug a hole and plunked in the grapevine, not at all sure it would survive. But it did. The next year, it shot runners all over the makeshift arbor and produced a luxuriant abundance of leaves—and a few measly grapes. I was disappointed. My jelly jars and I were all ready to put up royal purple grape jelly. Instead, the children and I ate about four grapes apiece and called it a year. The next spring, armed with a gardening book, pruning shears, and high hopes, I set to work on the little vine. I learned that grapevines produce two kinds of branches: producing and nonproducing. The trick was to determine which was which.

With amateur skill and great enthusiasm, I hacked away. When I was finished, my husband stroked his chin, regarded the vine's sorry state, and asked, "Have you called the funeral home to make arrangements?"

But to everyone's surprise, not least of all my own, that year the little vine bore grapes! Not a great abundance, but considering its tender age and unpromising beginnings, I was impressed. Each subsequent year, I got better at pruning, and it got better at bearing grapes. A little fertilizer here, a little bug killer there, and the harvests began to be substantial.

As I worked on my grapevine, training the fruit-bearing limbs on the arbor and snipping off the nonbearing branches, I often thought about Jesus tending the wild tendrils of my life. I mused about His high hopes for my fruit-bearing potential, and I shamefacedly realized He was no doubt often disappointed by my crop of bug-ridden, disease-prone spiritual fruit.

And then something occurred to me: The major difference between me and the branches on my little grapevine was this: I had a choice about how attached to the True Vine I wanted to be, while my little grapevine did not. Its branches wholeheartedly clung to the vine and just naturally bore fruit as a result. On the other hand, I choose how much life-giving, fruit-producing Holy Spirit sap I want flowing to my leaf buds.

The seeds of faith in my heart can only be nourished if I stay open to the work of the Spirit in my heart and life. Apart from God, I will wither and die. In Him, the seeds of faithfulness will flourish and grow strong.

But the fruit of the Spirit is. . . faithfulness.

GALATIANS 5:22 NIV

Faithfulness to Jesus Christ is the supernatural work of redemption that has been performed in me by the Holy Spirit—"the love of God has been poured out in our hearts by the Holy Spirit. . ." (Romans 5:5 NKJV). And it is that love in me that effectively works through me and comes in contact with everyone I meet. I remain faithful to His name, even though the commonsense view of my life may seemingly deny that, and may appear to be declaring that He has no more power than the morning mist.

OSWALD CHAMBERS

Faith. . .

is itself a supernatural act

of the human intellect,

and is thus a divine gift.

MORTIMER ADLER

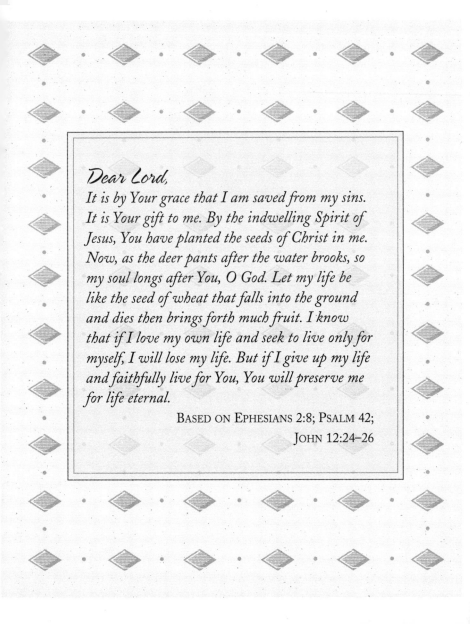

Dear Lord,

*It is by Your grace that I am saved from my sins.
It is Your gift to me. By the indwelling Spirit of
Jesus, You have planted the seeds of Christ in me.
Now, as the deer pants after the water brooks, so
my soul longs after You, O God. Let my life be
like the seed of wheat that falls into the ground
and dies then brings forth much fruit. I know
that if I love my own life and seek to live only for
myself, I will lose my life. But if I give up my life
and faithfully live for You, You will preserve me
for life eternal.*

BASED ON EPHESIANS 2:8; PSALM 42;
JOHN 12:24–26

Chapter 3

Little Sprouts

A man is not justified by observing the law, but by faith in Jesus Christ. So we, too, have put our faith in Jesus Christ that we may be justified by faith in Christ.

GALATIANS 2:16 NIV

Little faith will bring your souls to Heaven, but great faith will bring Heaven to your souls.

CHARLES H. SPURGEON

Faith That Grows into Faithfulness

Faith is God's gift to us, a seed of grace planted in our hearts. But now that new beginning must grow, sending out shoots of life, young leaves that burst into the sunlight. If we want to grow in our faith, then we need to get to know our God, for we will trust Him more as we know Him better.

I was standing with a friend at his garden gate one evening when two children came by. As they approached us he said to me: "Watch the difference in these two boys."

Taking one of them in his arms, he stood him on the gatepost, and stepping back a few feet, he folded his arms and called to the little fellow to jump. In an instant, the boy sprang toward him and was caught in his arms. Then turning to the second boy he tried the same experiment. But in the second case it was different. The child trembled and refused to move. My friend held out his arms and tried to induce the child to trust his strength, but nothing could move him. At last my friend had to lift him down from the post and let him go.

"What makes such a difference in the two?" I asked.

My friend smiled and said, "The first is my own boy and knows me; but the other is a stranger's child whom I have never seen before."

There was all the difference. My friend was equally able to prevent both from falling, but the difference was in the boys themselves. The first had assurance in his father's ability and acted upon it. . . .

So it is with us. We hesitate to trust ourselves to the loving One whose plans for us are higher than any we have ourselves made. He, too, with outstretched arms, calls us.   D. L. MOODY

If we spend time with the Father, learning to trust Him, we will not be afraid to leap into His arms.

A Tiny Seed That Sprouted
A Small Basket of Faith

With some trepidation, the little boy laid his small woven lunch basket into Jesus' hands then looked up into His smiling face. Like most children, he liked to help, and he'd overheard the disciples discussing their problem. There was a big crowd of people and Jesus told the disciples to feed them. But when the disciples looked at his lunch, they had scoffed. Would Jesus?

Jesus unlatched the basket and looked inside. Nestled together were five stale, none-too-clean barley buns and two fingerling fishes. Jesus grinned, almost laughed out loud, and shook His head.

"The faith of a child!" He said wonderingly.

The boy, ducking his head in embarrassment, twisted his stubbed great toe into the sand, and felt red-hot shame rising from his shoulders to the roots of his hair.

"Come here, lad," Jesus called to the boy. He extended His callused carpenter's hand and the boy placed his own small one into it.

"Thank you," Jesus said, looking directly into the boy's eyes.

Jesus and the disciples gazed down the side of the mountain. Among the rocks, the crowd of about 5,000 men plus twice again that many women and children had dispersed into little clusters. Small children who had been presented to Jesus with twisted limbs now danced and played on sound legs. The skin of the lepers was smooth, whole, and restored. The formerly blind were marveling over a world they had previously only seen through their fingertips.

"Have the people sit on the ground," Jesus told His disciples.

Quickly, the word spread up the hillside and the crowd eagerly sat down facing Jesus. Perhaps Jesus was going to teach again. Perhaps heal. An expectant hush fell over the people.

Still holding the child's hand, He looked up into heaven as if He could see the very face of God. "Thank You," He said again very simply, and the boy didn't know if Jesus was thanking God for his lunch or him.

Perhaps it was for both.

Jesus tore a piece from one of the loaves and dropped the bit into a nearby basket. Then He tore it again and again and again and again.

Inexplicably, the basket filled. As the torn pieces of bread reached the top of the basket, the amazed silence had grown so heavy that when Jesus quietly asked for another basket, His voice could be heard to the back edges of the crowd.

His request spurred the stunned disciples back to life.

"Another basket!" one of the disciples called out and it was produced.

Jesus repeated the process with a fish. And then another loaf. And then a fish. There seemed to be no end until every stomach was filled and there were twelve baskets full of leftovers.

It is not so much the size of the gift that matters to Jesus, because in His hands a small lunch can effortlessly become a mighty banquet. The importance is that it is given in faith.

A Living Miracle

Most mothers are concerned when their children are sick, but Jenny Miller had a special worry when sixteen-month-old Amber was ill for a week with intestinal problems. Not long before, one of the Millers' other children had been stricken with cancer, and now Jenny was worried that Amber had it, too.

"She wouldn't eat or drink anything," said Jenny. "And I'd seen those scrawny-looking arms before." They reminded her of the way cancer had affected her other daughter. As panic set in, Jenny reminded herself, *I need to trust the Lord.*

Amber's doctor examined her and concluded her problem was simple dehydration. He recommended that Jenny take her daughter to the emergency room for intravenous fluids.

Although Amber had been weak and listless, Jenny, two emergency room nurses, and a male orderly had to wrap Amber in a sheet and hold her down while they tried to start an IV. As the child screamed in anger and pain, they stuck her tiny, dehydrated veins twelve times in different areas without success. Finally, they gave up, deciding to call someone from the pediatric floor to start the IV.

Alone with her sobbing child, Jenny bowed her head over Amber. "Lord, I don't know how much more poking I can stand. I need a miracle," said Jenny. "I need someone to come in, do one poke, and be done."

At that moment, a soft-spoken nurse entered the examining room. She calmly soothed the tiny girl and looked for a likely place to start the IV. "I think there's a vein here in her forehead that might work," said the nurse.

This time, other restraining hands were not needed. Jenny

held Amber in her arms as the young woman leaned over and quickly, efficiently inserted the needle.

Jenny's eyes fell on the nurse's name badge, and she smiled as she let out a long sigh of relief. God had sent an answer to her prayer.

"Lisa Miracle," the name badge read.

Faith is sometimes equated with credulity, but it can be so equated only when the profound mistake is made of thinking of faith as primarily a matter of intellectual assent. As the New Testament uses the word, faith is trust, acceptance, commitment, vision. It is not a belief in this or that creed; it is a quality which lies rather in the realm of intuition than the intellect. Faith has indeed an element of true simplicity; it is one of the qualities— perhaps the fundamental quality—of the childlike spirit without which no man can enter the Kingdom of God.

Anonymous

A HARVEST OF FAITHFULNESS

Words To Help Us Grow
Even in the Shifting Sands of Life

- When I don't have the answer, God is the Answer.
- When the storms of life threaten to shipwreck me, Jesus is my Anchor.
- When I am lost, God is omnipresent.
- When I am weak, God is strong.
- When I need shelter, God is my Refuge.
- When I die, God is Life.
- When I am afraid, God is my Father.
- When I am sinful, Jesus is my Sacrifice.
- When I doubt, God is faithful.
- When I am besieged, God is my Shield.
- When I am in the dark, Jesus is my Light.
- When I am lost, Jesus is the Way.
- When I am sinking, God holds me in His hand.
- When the shifting sands threaten to bury me, God is a firm Foundation.

Faith is our spiritual oxygen.
It not only keeps us alive in God,
but enables us to
grow stronger.

JOYCE LANDORF HEATHERLY

Growing!
Activities to Enhance Your Faithfulness

◆ Start a prayer journal. Use a spiral-bound note-book or a diary, and enter into it all your praises and requests. Be sure to leave room to note the date each time you pray for a specific request. When the Lord answers your prayer, record the answer—and celebrate!

◆ Be a faithful witness by sharing your answers to prayer with others.

- Plan a date with God. In addition to your regular daily devotional time, plan an occasional lunch alone with the Lord. Find someplace where you won't be disturbed, take your Bible and a sandwich, and spend the hour admiring God. Don't ask for anything! Just enjoy what He's already done for you!

- Designate a verse for the day. Jot it down on a 3 x 5 card and keep it where you can refer to it while your computer is booting up or while you perform other daily chores.

But without faith
it is impossible to please him:
for he that cometh to God
must believe that he is,
and that he is a rewarder of them
that diligently seek him.

HEBREWS 11:6

Faith means being zealous for God: in pious ignorance and intellectual darkness, without understanding, without feeling, without thinking, waiting upon God's activity.

Christ is the object of faith, nay, rather, not the object, but it may be said, the subject, the One present and active in the faith itself.

Though our faith may be weak, let us pray earnestly in company with the apostles, "Lord, increase our faith" (Luke 17:5), and with the father of the child in Mark 9:24, "Lord, I believe; help thou my unbelief."

MARTIN LUTHER

Sprouting Faithful Reliance
High-Octane Grace When Life Seems Out of Control

"Cars puzzle me," said Catherine. "All I know is if you put in gas, they are supposed to start. When they don't, I have no clue what to do." Fortunately, Catherine's husband is mechanically inclined; however, even he was mystified when one day her car battery went dead.

"No spark, no nothing," said Catherine.

After tinkering with it for a while, Jim gave the car a jump, and the battery recharged. Thinking it was a fluke, neither gave the battery a second thought until a week later when Catherine drove to a suburb of Chicago on business. Low on gas, she found herself in a run-down area and was forced to stop.

Wire mesh covered the gas station windows, and a Doberman patrolled the interior. Behind a barred window, the attendant counted out Catherine's change, shoving it through a tiny slot.

Back in the car, Catherine locked her car doors and inserted the key in the ignition. She turned the key, but there was only a click. She tried again; this time there was no response whatsoever.

At this point, Catherine's mind wrote a headline for her hometown newspaper: "Local Woman's Corpse Found in Chicago Suburb."

"I was scared. This was no place to have car trouble. I bowed my head and prayed for wisdom. And then it was almost as though God told me what to do. I shut off the radio and the air conditioning and tried again."

The car roared to life.

"Now I know two things about cars," said Catherine. "They are powered by gas and the grace of God."

It is wrong to suppose that for Paul faith is a meritorious act on man's part, which wins salvation, or even, in a more modern way of speech, a creative moral principle in itself. Paul does not, in fact, speak (when he is using the language strictly) of "justification by faith," but of "justification by grace through faith," or "on the grounds of faith." This is not mere verbal subtlety. It means that the "righteousness of God" becomes ours, not by the assertion of the individual will as such, but by the willingness to let God work.

C. HAROLD DODD
The Meaning of Paul for Today

Dependent on God

The grapevine cannot make itself grow; it can only respond to the sun and the rain and the rich earth. In the same way, we cannot force our faith to grow; we can only turn toward God, allowing ourselves to respond to His nourishing grace at work in our lives.

A HARVEST OF FAITHFULNESS

Let your faith now lay hold of a new power in Christ. You have trusted Him as your dying Saviour; now trust Him as your living Saviour. Just as much as He came to deliver you from future punishment did He also come to deliver you from present bondage. Just as truly as He came to bear your stripes for you has He come to live your life for you. You are as utterly powerless in the one case as the other. You could as easily have got yourself rid of your own sins, as you could now accomplish for yourself practical righteousness. Christ, and Christ only, must do both for you; and your part in both cases is simply to give the thing to Him to do, and then believe that He does it.

HANNAH WHITALL SMITH

Dear Lord,
Help me to be faithful in the small things so
that I may be increasingly faithful as You trust
me with more. The words I most want to hear
from Your lips are, "Well done, good and
faithful servant: You have been faithful over a
few things so I have made you responsible
over many things. Enter into My joy!"

Based on LUKE 16: 11;
MATTHEW 25:21

Chapter 4

Sending Down Deep Roots

As ye have therefore received Christ Jesus the Lord,
so walk ye in him: Rooted and built up in him,
and stablished in the faith.
Colossians 2:6–7

You can keep a faith only as
you can keep a plant,
by rooting it into your life
and making it grow there.

Phillips Brooks

Our faith cannot be something that comes and goes. Instead, it must be deeply rooted in our identities—so that we will be deeply rooted in Christ. A grapevine does not wake up some mornings and say, "Today I don't think I feel like growing." No, it simply grows, moment by moment, so long as its roots are connected to a source of nourishment. Our faith in Christ should be the same.

> *That Christ may dwell in your hearts by faith;*
> *that ye, being rooted and grounded in love,*
> *may be. . .filled with all the fulness of God.*
> EPHESIANS 3:17–19

Faithful Roots
William Carey—A Faithful Plodder

Young William Carey was a proponent of an idea that was revolutionary to most eighteenth-century religious leaders: He believed that the Church was responsible for foreign evangelism. His position drew a fiery response from one of them: "Young man. . .when God pleases to convert the heathen, He will do it without your aid or mine!"

Some men and women would have been intimidated by this reaction. But Carey refused to be silenced. His study of the Bible forced him to the conclusion that missions was not an option but a duty. In 1794, at age thirty-two, he sailed for Calcutta, India, with his wife, Dorothy, their children, and another missionary family.

The five-month voyage was exceptionally difficult, fraught with storms and misery. Once they reached India, their troubles only grew worse. In addition to the language and cultural barrier, Carey's missionary companion was wholly unreliable with money, and he occasionally lapsed into periods of insanity. Their funds were soon depleted, they were harassed by the East Indian Company, and their group suffered a variety of physical afflictions.

When Carey's son Peter died, Dorothy Carey also became psychotic. For thirteen years until her death, she raged at Carey in her delirium while he worked to translate the Scriptures into Bengali.

Carey labored six years before he claimed his first soul for Christ. But by the time of his death some forty years later, he had baptized more than 1,500 new believers and taught thousands more in classes and services. He had also translated the Bible into six different languages, including Bengali. Together with his missionary compatriots, he translated the New Testament into twenty-three other languages as well, with portions translated and distributed in many other tongues. Carey's faithfulness served as an inspiration to many, and from his influence grew dozens of missionary societies.

However, Carey did not see himself as extraordinary. To his nephew Eustace he wrote: "If, after my removal, anyone should think it worth his while to write my life, I will give you a criterion by which you may judge of its correctness. If he gives me credit for being a plodder, he will describe me justly. Anything beyond this will be too much. I can plod. I can persevere in any definite pursuit. To this I owe everything."

We like to think of faithfulness in terms of adventure and great heroic actions. But when we're truly rooted in Christ, we'll see the truth: Sometimes plodding forward is all we need to do to demonstrate our faithfulness.

The future is as bright as the promises of God.

WILLIAM CAREY

Waiting On the Lord

When Steve and Lisa's daughter Clancy was born with a small hole in her heart, the doctors encouraged them to have it stitched shut soon because "little ones recover so quickly."

However, the procedure was drastic and they didn't feel right about the risks. The surgeons would split open her breastbone to expose the heart and make her vulnerable to massive infection. Afterwards, she would bear a large scar the length of her torso.

Said Lisa: "We were certainly not against surgery, but we figured since we served the Creator, perhaps He wanted to heal her supernaturally."

For the first five years of Clancy's life, they waited and watched and prayed. Somehow, they still didn't feel a peace about scheduling the surgery even though there was no change in her condition.

"We assumed," said Lisa, "that God was going to answer our prayers and show His miraculous power as a testimony to Clancy and those around her. How small-minded of us! God had something much more intimate and personal in mind."

When an EKG during the summer of 1998 showed no change, they set the surgery's date for October. While they were a little surprised God had not healed her, they were "rejoicing in all things" and trusting God to work everything out in His own way.

"Try to tell a mother that open-heart surgery on her

daughter is routine and see if she believes you," said Lisa. "They did and I didn't! But it turned out to be true."

Four days after the surgery, Clancy was home petting her dog. But that was not what amazed Lisa and Steve: It was the new surgical procedure that was used on Clancy. Just a year and a half earlier, a new method had been developed and the doctor employed this on Clancy. Far less invasive, it left nothing more than a small three-inch scar beneath her right breast and greatly minimized the risk of infection and complications.

"There will be no visible indication that she was born with anything but a 'whole' heart," said Lisa. "Does it touch you as much as it does us that God would care how a young girl would feel about her body? He knew that we needed a message about what a tender, loving Father we have. We trusted Him to tell us when to have the surgery, and His timing was absolutely perfect!"

I thought on my ways,
and turned my feet
unto thy testimonies.
I made haste, and delayed not
to keep thy commandments.

PSALM 119:59-60

A HARVEST OF FAITHFULNESS

Be dependable. If God has called you to a task, continue it until He tells you otherwise. This is beautifully expressed in the following poem by an unknown African American author.

There's a King and a Captain high,
And He's coming by and by,
And He'll find me hoeing cotton when He comes.
You can hear His legions charging in the regions of
    the sky,
And He'll find me hoeing cotton when He comes.
There's the Man they thrust aside,
Who was tortured till He died,
And He'll find me hoeing cotton when He comes.
He was hated and rejected,
He was scorned and crucified,
And He'll find me hoeing cotton when He comes.
When He comes! When He comes!
He'll be crowned by saints and angels when He comes.
They'll be shouting out Hosanna! To the Man that
    men denied,
And I'll kneel among my cotton when He comes.

AUTHOR UNKNOWN

We see this sort of faithfulness in the man who planted a crop of walnut trees. It took twenty years for them to grow deep roots and reach maturity—but when they did, their harvest made the wait well worthwhile!

The roots of your faith are grounded in the hope of eternity. So it makes sense to expect the reward for your faithfulness in Heaven.

> *All virtue consists in having a willing heart; God will lead you by the hand, if only you do not doubt, and are filled with love for Him rather than fear for yourself.*
>
> FRANCOIS DE FÉNELON

Exposure to Sonshine—Prayer Time

One of the best ways to become deeply rooted in faith is through simply spending time with God, your heart open to Him. Prayer is a tender, precious, loving time between you and your Lord. It stirs your roots and makes you lift your leaves to the nourishing warmth of His presence. By spending this quality time with Him, you become empowered and healed. You will bring about eternal changes in your life and in the lives of others by spending time in prayer. You can't spend time with God without coming away as a different person.

Jesus was God's Son, but that didn't mean He didn't need to make the time for special moments alone with His Father. He took time to be with God. The disciples were so impressed with the vitality of His prayer life that they asked Him to teach them how to pray as well. He gave them an example, "The Lord's Prayer" (Matthew 6:9–13), a model you too can follow.

Here's a breakdown of Jesus' prayer:

- Our Father, who art in Heaven.

   This section of the prayer reminds us of our relationship to God and God's relationship to us. He is not only "our Father" who loves and tenderly cares for His children, but He is the heavenly Father, all-knowing, all-seeing, and all-powerful. Our faith is rooted in His identity.

- Hallowed be Thy name.

   This phrase reminds us to praise God's holy name. Through praise we draw close to God, and

He in turn draws close to us. We can't help but absorb the world's way of looking at things; to counteract this limited vision, we all need to spend time recognizing and appreciating God's holiness, sovereignty, love, faithfulness, and beauty. We do not praise God to butter Him up before we make our requests. Instead, praise helps us recognize who He is, thereby increasing our faith.

◆ Thy kingdom come. Thy will be done.

This is one of the most helpful, life-changing phrases in the prayer! What is God's kingdom? It is where God reigns. If He is Lord of our lives, then His kingdom is within us. His kingdom is in our homes. His kingdom is wherever we are, whenever we seek to make Him Lord. Therefore, we need to seek His will for each request we bring before the throne of God. How should we pray for our mates? Our children? Our employers? Our churches? When we seek God's best for ourselves and those around us, we cannot pray meaningless or selfish prayers. Instead, the Holy Spirit will prompt us to ask for help that will go to the heart of the matter. Asking that God's will be done also enables Him to change our minds about what is important. Suddenly, we see how much we need God to soften our own hearts— rather than simply telling God to teach that old so-and-so a lesson. As we realize God's involvement in our lives, our faith will grow.

♦ Give us this day our daily bread.

Here is where we make our requests for our own everyday needs. Of course, God knows before we ask, but when we do ask, He can do exceedingly, abundantly more than we ask or think (Ephesians 3:20).

♦ And forgive us our trespasses as we forgive our trespassers.

Confession of sins and shortcomings is an important aspect of our prayer life. Here is where we tell God where we have slipped up, the harmful attitudes we have fostered, and where our souls need reinforcements against enemy aggression. As we confess our sins to God, we can more easily forgive those who have offended or sinned against us. Forgiveness is a vital part of our growth in faith.

- And lead us not into temptation, but deliver us from evil.

Each of us has weak areas, and as we open our lives to the Holy Spirit, He will point out where He needs to strengthen our souls. Maybe our weaknesses are in the area of self-discipline, gluttony, or lust; wherever we are weak, by admitting our need, we open our lives to God's help and deliverance. Although Jesus encouraged His disciples to pray in the Garden of Gethsemane on the night He was betrayed (Mark 14:38), they neglected to do this. As a result, they had little power against temptation and not much courage. Their faith was at an all-time low.

- For thine is the kingdom, the power, and the glory forever.

This final line of Jesus' prayer helps us to put our lives into perspective with who God really is—the omnipotent and all-glorious King.

Disciples of Jesus! who have asked the Master to teach you to pray, come now and accept His lessons. He tells you that prayer is the path to faith, strong faith, that can cast out devils. He tells you, "If ye have faith, nothing shall be impossible to you"; let this glorious promise encourage you to pray much. Is the prize not worth the price? Shall we not give up all to follow Jesus in the path He opens to us here. . . ? Shall we not do anything that neither the body nor the world around hinder us in our great lifework— having intercourse with our God in prayer, that we may become men of faith, whom He can use in His work. . . ?

ANDREW MURRAY

Faith never knows where it is being led or it would not be faith. True faith is content to travel under sealed orders.

J. OSWALD SANDERS

Strengthening Your Root System
Orange Blossoms After the Pruning

During Sarah's freshman year in college, she made three inseparable girlfriends who spent their days hanging around together and having fun. Their carefree days were cut short by tragedy after the second semester:

On June 24, 1989, one of the girls, Melissa, was missing and suspected to be the victim of a murder. For the next week while police searched, the three remaining friends waited tensely and prayed.

Said Sarah: "I was experimenting with alcohol at the time. I know you're not supposed to bargain with God, but I wanted to make a sacrificial gift, like Hannah offering Samuel, so He would understand how serious I was.

"So I told Him, 'If you can produce her body—dead or alive —so her family can have some closure, I'll give up drinking.'"

When two days later Melissa's body was recovered, Sarah did not forget her promise to God. The horror of Melissa's death and the urging of the Holy Spirit would not let her.

"Every year, when June 24 rolled around, I would be really sad. The memory was so painful," said Sarah.

No longer involved in drinking parties, Sarah met Tim, a Christian man and musician. They fell in love and eventually set a wedding date.

In 1995, on her wedding day, Sarah remembers thinking:

"This is the happiest day of my life!" Then a bell rang in her mind: It was not only the happiest day; it was the saddest, too. The date was June 24—the anniversary of Melissa's death.

"I wasn't thinking about her death when I set the wedding date," said Sarah, "but God used her death to change the course of my life. I didn't become a barfly. I didn't end up meeting some sleaze-bag guy in a bar and marrying him. I met a Christian man instead.

"When you are faithful to God and your commitment to Him, He blesses you in ways that you'd never guess."

Faithful Dependence on God

"When you hear your child, fresh from the hands of God, has a birth defect, it makes you want to scream with the unfairness of it all," said Phyllis. For a while after their son's diagnosis, Phyllis was severely depressed. "I'm normally an upbeat sort of person. But when the diagnosis came down, I just bottomed out. I quit reading my Bible and praying. I was giving God the silent treatment!"

Her husband Mark said that the diagnosis made him search the Scriptures for answers. "I kept noticing that God told us to rejoice in all things—including troubles and temptations—when we make our requests known to Him. It dawned on me that perhaps God told us to do that for two reasons: When we acknowledge the almighty, all-powerful attributes of God, we are empowered to have more faith in Him when we make our requests. But, first and foremost, praising God in a time of trouble is an act of faithful obedience to Him. He honors that."

When Mark first shared his discoveries with Phyllis, she reacted with hostility. "I thought he was getting 'holier-than-thou.' But over time, when I saw what a change this new attitude made in the way Mark approached our son and the decisions we had to make concerning him, I realized I was seeing the supernatural peace and grace of God. I for sure wasn't getting that from the antidepressants I was taking, so I decided to quit Prozac and start praising!"

While Mark and Phyllis still struggle with their son's many disabilities, they have seen God do some miraculous things in their lives. "Our son is progressing far better than the doctors said he ever could," said Phyllis. "We know God has shown us what to do in each area of treatment. And God has opened up a ministry for us with other parents of severely handicapped children.

"When they say to us, 'How are you holding up?' we can say, 'By the grace of God!' Then we share with them what He has done for us and our son."

God didn't call us to be successful, just faithful.

MOTHER TERESA

Rooted in Faithfulness

Although the temperatures during the winter of 1939 were especially frigid, Carl and Catherine remember that year with special warmth.

As pastors of a very small church in northern Illinois, they lived in a drafty parsonage heated only by a coal stove. Although they didn't mind being chilly themselves, they worried about their six-month-old firstborn son. This was the heart of the Great Depression, and the church paid only a small, token salary. There simply wasn't enough money to supply their most basic needs.

"With our last fuel in the heating stove," said Carl, "we knelt for our prayer time and asked God to provide us with some coal. As we prayed, we heard the mailman's feet crunching on the snow on our wooden porch."

After they finished with their prayer time, they collected their mail—a single letter. Upon opening it, they read the following:

We thought maybe you needed some money to keep the baby warm. Don't thank us. It's some of the Lord's money.

"We still have the letter," said Carl. "We were reminded of the verse, 'And it shall come to pass, that before they call, I will answer; and while they are yet speaking, I will hear' " (Isaiah 65:24).

Their baby survived that cold winter, and he is now a missionary.

Growing Roots

When our world is shaking and pieces of our lives are falling around us, then we need to wrap our roots around the Solid Rock and cling. But when the jarring ceases—and it will stop—we discover that we were not so much holding on to the Rock, but that He was holding on to us.

Dear Lord,
You are my God. Early will I seek You. My soul
thirsts for You; my flesh longs for You in this dry
and thirsty world where there is no water. Why
should my soul be cast down? Why should my
spirit be disquietedwithin me? I will hope in You:
I shall praise You, for You put the smile on my

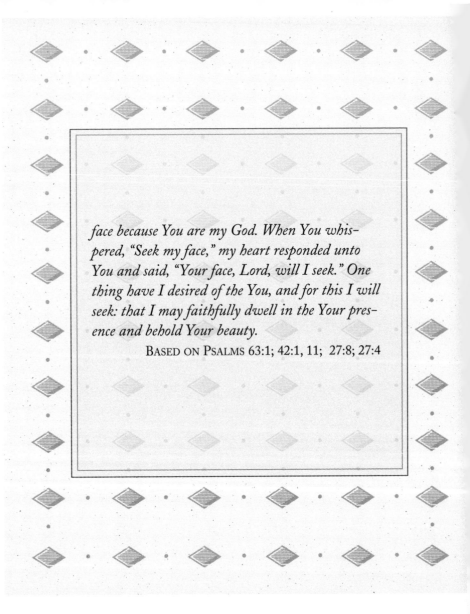

face because You are my God. When You whis-
pered, "Seek my face," my heart responded unto
You and said, "Your face, Lord, will I seek." One
thing have I desired of the You, and for this I will
seek: that I may faithfully dwell in the Your pres-
ence and behold Your beauty.

BASED ON PSALMS 63:1; 42:1, 11; 27:8; 27:4

Chapter 5

Pruning and Weeding

[Jesus said,] "I am the true vine, and my Father is the gardener. He cuts off every branch in me that bears no fruit, while every branch that does bear fruit he prunes so that it will be even more fruitful. . . . Remain in me, and I will remain in you. "No branch can bear fruit by itself; it must remain in the vine. Neither can you bear fruit unless you remain in me.

"I am the vine; you are the branches. If a man remains in me and I in him, he will bear much fruit; apart from me you can do nothing. If anyone does not remain in me, he is like a branch that is thrown. . .into the fire and burned.

"If you remain in me and my words remain in you, ask whatever you wish, and it will be given you. This is to my Father's glory, that you bear much fruit, showing yourselves to be my disciples."   JOHN 15:1–2, 3–8 NIV

All of us have times when our lives need to be weeded of sin, times when even the lovely things in our lives must be pruned so that we can grow strong and whole in Christ. The process hurts—but God wants us to become all that He created us to be.

Faithfully Trusting in God's Goodness During a Severe Pruning

It wasn't until I was a parent that I realized how much it pains God to have to discipline us.

My daughter was a strong, wiry baby, and by the time she was seven months old, she could scoot herself all over the house. Her favorite toy was the broiler pan at the base of the kitchen range. She saw herself reflected in the chrome, then would pull down the door to watch the pilot light. She soon discovered she could squeeze herself inside, near that intriguing, dancing flame.

As a first-time mama, I had never before had to discipline

my own child. With visions of my baby burnt to a crisp or asphyxiated, my initial instinct was to block shut the broiler pan or distract her with other toys, but she was determined to play with the flame. When "No! No!" didn't work, I very reluctantly and softly patted her small fingers.

But gentle pats were no deterrent to my little explorer. She merely looked offended and went back to the boiler pan.

With a breaking heart, I swatted her tiny hand hard enough to sting. Now she truly was aggrieved. Her china-blue eyes flooded with tears as her indignant cries filled the house. She could not understand why I would not let her play with the fire; she only knew I was a mean, mean mother.

This proved to be only the opening foray in a long battle to protect her from maiming or killing herself before she reached maturity and understanding. At any time, I would have willingly died to protect this little girl; she had no idea how much I hurt when I caused her pain for her own good. With tears streaming down my face, I stroked and comforted my wayward baby. She quickly forgot her pain, but I still bear the scars of it on my heart.

We have a Heavenly Father who knows when we lose a hair. He is certainly aware of every twinge we feel, yet He is willing to hurt time and time again for our own good, to protect us from the flames of life that look as charming and harmless as a pilot light to a baby.

You may think you're the only one in the world to suffer wearisome pruning. You may believe that your only real balm is licking the sores of your soul. You may feel very alone. However, at these times, you are actually receiving the personal attention of the Master Gardener. Nothing haphazard is being done to you. Every bit of pruning is important and necessary.

You may doubt God's intentions during a pruning phase —but He can create good even out of the evil things in life. Trust Him to do what is best for you. Out of this pain will come healthy growth.

You may be angry with God for allowing trouble to come into your life. After all, you may ask, if He loved you, why would He allow you to suffer? But remember: He permitted His own perfect Son to suffer the same sort of afflictions we suffer. While you may not be able to relax during the pain, take advantage of it as an opportunity to work with God. Take courage in God's love.

Faithfulness is required when we don't understand what God is doing in our lives, when He allows something to occur that we find puzzling, indefensible, or downright cruel. Our confused minds ask our hearts, "Are you still going to trust God?"

The faithful heart will answer a resounding, "Yes!"

Under the Heavenly Pruning Knife
Faithful Submission

When Mary found a cancerous lump in her breast, she said, "I thought I was cool and I was faithfully trusting God for everything." But despite her brave exterior, Mary was being eaten alive with fear.

"I feared I was going to be like my mother who died of brain cancer. Everything she tried made her sicker." Mary also worried about what would befall her young daughter if she should die. Determined to find healing by any method other than mastectomy, she traveled long distances to investigate alternative cancer treatments. But when another lump appeared, Mary relinquished all pretense of serenity. Frightened, bombarded with a bewildering assortment of conventional and alternative cancer treatments and diets, she sat in her car in the doctor's parking lot and prayed, "Lord, You've got to tell me what to do. I know the doctor is going to say I need the breast removed."

The Lord brought Proverbs 8:33 and Proverbs 19:20 to her mind. Curious as to what the verses would say, Mary flipped through her Bible and read Proverbs 8:33: "Listen to my instruction and be wise; do not ignore it" (NIV). Then she read Proverbs 19:20: "Listen to advice and accept instruction, and in the end you will be wise" (NIV).

When the needle biopsy revealed more cancer, she felt the

Lord's leading to go through surgery. "I had incredible peace," said Mary. "After it was over, God showed me that He was going to love me in ways I never had experienced. People came out of the woodwork to help me. Today, for the first time, I know my husband loves me just the way I am.

"To have fear is to not trust God. But in Him, I am made perfect and complete, lacking nothing. I'm healthy today—but I needed cancer to teach me what true faithfulness really is."

Have courage for
the great sorrows of life
and patience for the small ones;
and when you have laboriously
accomplished your daily task,
go to sleep in peace.
God is awake.

VICTOR HUGO

Abiding in the Vine

How do you and I produce a harvest of faithfulness? By abiding in the True Vine, willingly submitting to whatever pruning the Master Gardener deems necessary (John 15:1–8).

How do we abide in—or remain connected to—the Vine? By letting the life-giving, fruit-producing Holy Spirit work in our lives.

Perennial Favorites
Faithful Truths to Live by When Life Is out of Your Control

*And we know that
in all things God works for
the good of those who love him,
who have been called
according to his purpose.*

ROMANS 8:28 NIV

So do not fear, for I am with you; do not be dismayed, for I am your God. I will strengthen you and help you; I will uphold you with my righteous right hand.

ISAIAH 41:10 NIV

Cast your cares on the LORD and he will sustain you; he will never let the righteous fall.

PSALM 55:22 NIV

"Consider the lilies how they grow: they toil not, they spin not; and yet I say unto you, that Solomon in all his glory was not arrayed like one of these.

"If then God so clothe the grass, which is to day in the field, and to morrow is cast into the oven; how much more will he clothe you, O ye of little faith?

"And seek not ye what ye shall eat, or what ye shall drink, neither be ye of doubtful mind.

"For all these things do the nations of the world seek after: and your Father knoweth that ye have need of these things.

"But rather seek ye the kingdom of God; and all these things shall be added unto you." LUKE 12:27–31

A HARVEST OF FAITHFULNESS

If anyone had reason to worry, it was the apostle Paul. As a leader of a severely persecuted church, he was hated by the influential Jews and under arrest by Roman authorities. He was to plead his case before Nero, one of the most vicious and insane men ever to rule Rome. Yet Paul wrote these thoughts: Don't worry about anything; but in everything that happens, with prayer and supplication, with thanksgiving, let your requests be made known to God. And the peace of God, which goes beyond all human thought, will stand sentinel over your hearts and minds in Christ Jesus (based on Philippians 4:6–7).

Here's how Paul recommends that we vanquish worry with faith:

Take everything to God. There is no problem too vast for God's power and nothing too trifling for His Fatherly care.

We can make requests of God. Us. You and me. We can approach the throne of the Almighty God of the universe and find grace and help in our time of need. We don't have to be anyone special.

*Every moment of worry
weakens the soul for
its daily combat.*

HENRY WOOD

Expect peace. This isn't simply the garden variety of peace such as the world gives, this is the supernatural peace of God, and it will protect your heart, mind, and health (Proverbs 3:5–6) in Christ Jesus.

Faith by its very nature must be tested and tried. And the real trial of faith is not that we find it difficult to trust God, but that God's character must be proven as trustworthy in our own minds. Faith being worked out into reality must experience times of unbroken isolation. Never confuse the trial of faith with the ordinary discipline of life, because a great deal of what we call the trial of faith is the inevitable result of being alive. Faith, as the Bible teaches it, is faith in God coming against everything that contradicts Him—a faith that says, "I will remain true to God's character whatever He may do." The highest and the greatest expression of faith in the whole Bible is— "Though He slay me, yet will I trust Him" (JOB 13:15 NKJV). OSWALD CHAMBERS

A HARVEST OF FAITHFULNESS

Wiping Out Leaf Diseases, Bugs, and Other Pests
Besetting Sins That Mar Faithfulness

It's a fact: Everyone sins. With the exception of Jesus, every soul who ever drew breath suffers in one way or another with the effects of sin.

The good news: The power of Jesus breaks the power of sin—every sin. Secret sins, big sins, little sins, addictive sins—you name them, Jesus nailed them to the cross and they are conquered.

The whole course of things
goes to teach us faith.
We need only obey.
There is guidance for
each of us.

RALPH WALDO EMERSON

Expect Pests!

Studying the Bible is a wonderful way to help pull the weeds out of your life—but it isn't necessarily easy. Expect distractions to grow around your Bible study times like wild, thorn-bearing vines.

The phone will ring; the kids will fight. Satan will kick up a dust storm of diversions. He doesn't want you to read the blessed report that outlines your inheritance and power as a child of the King. He'd rather you remained weak and ignorant.

Satan will also seek to prevent you from studying God's word by whispering that you can't possibly understand the Bible. But know this: The same Holy Spirit who inspired the pens of the writers of the Scripture will quicken your mind in Christ Jesus, revealing the truth of His Word.

Pulling Up the Little Weeds Before They Get Established
Admitting Our Temptations

When we pray the Lord's Prayer, we admit that we are prone to temptation. In other words, we are bunglers with weaknesses that have the potential to destroy our lives and keep us from fulfilling God's purpose for us. In the Garden of Gethsemane, the disciples clearly showed their weakness: They slept, satiated by a big meal, their flesh satisfied, while Jesus agonized. What Jesus asked of them was not as important to them as a short nap.

How important is your prayer time?

> *Being faithful to Jesus Christ is the most difficult thing we try to do today. We will be faithful to our work, to serving others, or to anything else; just don't ask us to be faithful to Jesus Christ. Many Christians become very impatient when we talk about faithfulness to Jesus. Our Lord is dethroned more deliberately by Christian workers than by the world. We treat God as if He were a machine designed only to bless us, and we think of Jesus as just another one of the workers.* OSWALD CHAMBERS

The LORD is my strength and my shield; my heart trusted in him, and I am helped.

PSALM 28:7

Enumerating our areas of weakness before God's throne does several important things for us:

- It sensitizes us to those potential breaches in our spiritual armor and calls in heavenly reinforcements to fortify them.

- It helps us to be watchful against attack.

- It humbles us, a great asset, because spiritual pride is a deadly sin in itself.

- It prepares us to admit our flaws to a brother or sister in Christ and ask them for prayer support.

Confessing our temptations prepares us for God's victory over the weakness. Once we recognize our need, we can ask for God's help—and receive it!

Walk boldly and wisely. . . .
There is a hand above
that will help thee on.

PHILIP JAMES BAILEY

A HARVEST OF FAITHFULNESS

Submitting to the Pruner's Shears
Celebrating God When in Trouble

It is easy to obey God's directions when you know what the future holds. But only God knows the future—which is why He's the One giving directions.

Rejoicing in adversity may be one of the hardest things we'll ever do—it certainly goes against our grain. When calamity comes our way, our human nature wants to reach into Heaven, grab God by His lapels, and demand, "What are You doing? Why are You picking on me?"

But the Bible is clear: The faithful way to handle adversity is to rejoice in the Lord while you ask for His help:

Rejoice in the Lord always. I will say it again: Rejoice! . . . Do not be anxious about anything, but in everything, by prayer and petition, with thanksgiving, present your requests to God. And the peace of God, which transcends all understanding, will guard your hearts and your minds in Christ Jesus.　　　　　　PHILIPPIANS 4:4, 6–7 NIV

Faith is not a storm cellar to which men and women can flee for refuge from the storms of life. It is, instead, an inner spiritual strength which enables them to face those storms with hope and serenity. . . . Faith has the miraculous power

to lift ordinary human beings to greatness in seasons of
stress. SAM ERVIN

You may be able to praise God when everything is fine, but are you faithful enough to praise Him when everything is a mess?

*But when he saw the wind, he was afraid and, beginning
to sink, cried out, "Lord, save me!" Immediately Jesus
reached out his hand and caught him. "You of little faith,"
he said, "why did you doubt?" And when they climbed
into the boat, the wind died down. Then those who were
in the boat worshiped him, saying, "Truly you are the Son
of God."* MATTHEW 14:30–33 NIV

Seasons of Uncertainty
When the Lions Roar

In the stillness of the night is when I most often hear the lions roar. Their roaring snaps me awake to find my nighttime world haunted by the grisly demons of fear and doubt. The lions are in the distance, but I can plainly hear them approaching. In my heart of hearts, I fear they will surround my frail hut of

A HARVEST OF FAITHFULNESS

grass, tear it down, and devour me.

"What if. . . ?" they taunt. "What if God doesn't love you? What if He does love you and decides to test you further by stealing one of your children? Your husband? Your health? You know that strange lump? It's cancer!"

As I try to resist the clamoring voices, they turn to a new topic. "Money! Money? You have no money, but you have bills! Your children will go wanting! They need new shoes now! And braces? Crooked teeth all their lives, and it will be all your fault! Your fault! The money you put in the church offering you stole from your children! You will be the laughingstock of your family and the whole town! God will help you? What if there is no God? No One to help? What if you are mistaken about God's call on your life and are heading down the wrong path? It's all a divine joke, you know. He really is just toying with you!

"What if. . . ? What if. . . ?"

There must be two people living inside me: The upbeat, daytime believer, full of faith and hope, and the frightened, pessimistic nighttime doubter.

Only one Word puts all my doubts to rest: Jesus! When I am faith*less,* He remains faith*full.*

Let nothing disturb thee; let nothing affright thee. All things are passing; God never changes. Patience gains all things; who has God wants nothing. God alone suffices.

TERESA OF AVILA

*Every sort of energy
and endurance,
of courage and capacity
for handling life's evils,
is set free in those
who have. . .faith.*

WILLIAM JAMES

The life of faith presents challenges that keep you going—and keep you growing! WARREN W. WIERSBE

Faith and Faithfulness in the Darkness

Faith is like the little night-light that burns in a sick-room; as long as it is there, the obscurity is not complete, we turn toward it and await the daylight.

ABBE HUVELIN

Even Jesus had His time of trial on the cross, a time of darkness when He could no longer sense His Father's presence. But it was in that terrible, dark moment, that He proved His faithfulness to the Father.

Every time you venture out in your life of faith, you will find something in your circumstances that, from a commonsense standpoint, will flatly contradict your faith. But common sense is not faith, and faith is not common sense. In fact, they are as different as the natural life and the spiritual. Can you trust Jesus Christ where your common sense cannot trust Him? Can you venture out with courage on the words of Jesus Christ, while the realities of your commonsense life continue to shout, "It's all a lie"? When you are on the mountaintop, it's easy to say, "Oh yes, I believe God can do it," but you have to come down from the mountain to the demon-possessed valley and face the realities that scoff at your Mount-of-Transfiguration belief (Luke 9:28–42). *Every time my theology becomes clear to my own mind, I encounter something that contradicts it. As soon as I say, "I believe 'God shall supply all [my] need,'" the testing of my faith begins* (Philippians 4:19 NKJV). *When my strength runs dry and my vision is blinded, will I endure this trial of my faith victoriously or will I turn back in defeat? Faith must be tested, because it can only become your intimate possession through conflict. What is challenging your faith right now? The test will either prove your faith right, or it will kill it. Jesus said, "Blessed is he who is not offended because of Me"* (Matthew 11:6 NKJV). *The ultimate thing is confidence in Jesus. "We have become partakers of Christ if we hold the beginning of our confidence steadfast to the end."* (Hebrews 3:14 NKJV). *Believe steadfastly on Him and everything that challenges you will strengthen your faith. There is continual testing in the life of faith up to the point of our physical death, which is the last great test. Faith is absolute trust in God—trust that could never imagine that He would forsake us (see Hebrews 13:5–6).*

OSWALD CHAMBERS
My Utmost for His Highest

This is the Faith of the Son of God. God withdrew, as it were, that the perfect Will of the Son might arise and go forth to find the Will of the Father.

GEORGE MACDONALD

Faith faces everything that makes the world uncomfortable —pain, fear, loneliness, shame, death—and acts with a compassion by which these things are transformed, even exalted.

SAMUEL H. MILLER

Faith sometimes falters,

because He does not

reward us immediately.

But hold out,

be steadfast,

bear the delay,

and you have carried the cross.

AUGUSTINE

You call for faith: I show you doubt, to prove that faith exists. The more of doubt, the stronger of faith, I say, If faith o'ercomes doubt. ROBERT BROWNING

Dormant But Not Dead
A Prayer for Faithfulness in the Desert of Affliction
(Based on Psalm 31)

Be merciful to me, Lord, for I am in distress. My eyes grow weak with sorrow; my soul and body are weak with grief. My life is consumed by anguish and my days with groaning. My strength fails because of my afflictions, and my bones grow weak.

Because of all my enemies, I am the utter contempt of my neighbors and a dread to my friends. Those who see me on the street flee from me. I hear the slander of many, and on every side, I feel terror. Enemies conspire against me and plot to take my life.

In You, Lord, I take refuge. Turn Your ear to me. Come quickly to my rescue. Be my refuge, a strong fortress to save me. Free me from the trap that is set for me.

Into Your hands, I commit my spirit. My times are in Your

hands. Deliver me from my enemies and those who pursue me. Let Your face shine on me.

How great is the goodness bestowed on me when I take refuge in You! In the shelter of Your presence You hide me. Praise to You, Lord, for You show Your wonderful love to me when I am besieged. Even though I cry, "I am cut off from Your sight!" You will hear my cry and take mercy on me.

Faith alone is able, under trial,

to hear the deep secret

"Yea" of God beneath

and above his "Nay."

MARTIN LUTHER

Reason is the greatest enemy that faith has: It never comes to the aid of spiritual things, but—more frequently than not—struggles against the divine Word, treating with contempt all that emanates from God.

MARTIN LUTHER

Faithfulness on Deep Waters

When you're sailing on life's ocean through deep and dangerous waters and you are surrounded by storms and high waves, remember these things to remain faithfully afloat:

- The God who separated the seas from the naked soil (Genesis 1:9–10) can set your feet on dry land.

- The God who told Noah how to build an ark when no one had ever seen one before (Genesis 6–8) will tell you what to do when your troubles surround you like a flood.

- The God who opened Hagar's eyes so she could find a well of water in a dry wilderness (Genesis 21:19) will reveal a refreshing oasis where you thought was only sand.

- The God who parted the Red Sea for the children of Israel when they were pursued by a well-equipped army (Exodus 14) will open a path for your escape.

- The God who told Moses how to sweeten the bitter waters of Marah (Exodus 15:22–26) will show you how to turn life's sourest offerings into moments of joy.

- The God who brought water out of a rock (Exodus 17:1–7) will nourish you through hard times.

- The God who parted the Jordan River to admit the Israelites into a land flowing with milk and honey (Joshua 3) will open a way to lead you into a new life.

- The Christ who changed water into wine (John 2:1–11) will bring richness to your soul.

- The Christ who taught Peter how to walk on water (Matthew 14:22–32) will empower you to step over your problems.

- The Christ who told the wind and waves to be still and they did (Luke 8:22–25) will speak peace to the storms in your heart.

In the moments when you can't hear God or feel God, hold fast to the truth that God is Love and Satan is a Liar (1 John 4:8; John 8:44).

Unthread the rude eye
of rebellion,
And welcome home again
discarded faith.

WILLIAM SHAKESPEARE

A Gardener Who Understands

When we go through times of trial and grief, we can comfort ourselves with this knowledge: Jesus understands our fear and sorrow.

Through Jesus, God knows. . .

- what it is to work for a living;
- to labor day after day to struggle to make ends meet;
- to have a difficult customer who is never satisfied . . .because Jesus worked in a carpentry shop.

Through Jesus, God knows. . .

- what it is like to live in a house with others;
- to see the illness and death of someone you love;
- to have to share;
- to have disagreements;
- to have your family disagree with you;
- to be concerned for the needs and future of your loved ones
  . . .because Jesus had brothers and sisters, a mother and a father.

Through Jesus, God knows. . .

- what it is like to be tempted;
- to long for fleshly comforts;
- to be hungry;

- to hurt;
- to be sorrowful;
- to cry;
- to be disappointed;
- to sweat;
- to be tired;
- to weep;
- to sing;
- to be happy;
- to be a child;
- to be an adolescent;
- to be a son;
- to be a brother;
- to die

    . . .because while He was fully God, He was completely human.

Through Jesus, God knows. . .

- what it is to sweat blood;
- to be betrayed by a close friend;
- to cry alone;
- to be misunderstood;
- to be abandoned;
- to have a best friend deny he ever knew you;

- to be beaten;
- to be publicly ridiculed;
- to be falsely accused;
- to be falsely convicted of a crime;
- to be executed for a crime you didn't commit;
- to die alone
  . . .because He loved us enough to give His life on the cross.

When we are loved so much by Christ, how can we help but love Him back? That love will keep our faith strong even when God allows times of painful pruning to enter our lives.

God is. . .
disciplining us and training us
that we may achieve stability
and certainty in the life of faith.
Let us learn our lessons
and let us stand fast.

A. B. SIMPSON

Whatever the reasons for our trouble, we must not allow our souls to become so overwhelmed that we think we have committed some "unpardonable sin." For out of all the terror comes the soothing voice of our Lord Himself, "Be of good cheer: it is I; be not afraid."

Too many disciples have faith in their faith, or in their joy in the Lord; and when a spiritual storm comes, they have neither faith nor joy. Only one thing can endure, and that is love for God. If such love is not there, we will not recognize the living voice of God when He cries out that He is our refuge and our strength, a very present help in trouble. OSWALD CHAMBERS

Reaping Direction For Your Life— Faithfully Seeking God's Way

North? South? East? West?

Long ago in the one-room schoolhouses, the blackboard was nearly always positioned on the north wall. This served two purposes: It added a little extra insulation between the cold north wind and the children—and it helped them become orientated to the compass directions. Children soon learned to "feel" north.

In those days, a popular "wiggle reducer" and learning aid often used by teachers was to have the students stand beside their desks with their eyes closed. The teacher would call out directions: "North. West. South. East. West." The children were to turn in the direction the teacher called out. When they opened their eyes, they could see if they actually had followed directions.

Why does God allow uncertainty and questioning in our life? So we become reoriented to God's direction for us. When we know we are heading the right way, we can run the race toward the high calling of God in Christ Jesus. We just want to be certain we are running in the right direction.

Faith in the Darkness

Suppose I have a sick boy. I know nothing about medicine; but I call in the doctor, and put that boy's life and everything into his hands. I do not fail to believe in him; and I do not interfere at all. Do you call that trusting in the dark? Not at all! I used my best judgment and I put that boy's life into the hands of a good physician.

You have a soul diseased. Put it into the hands of the Great Physician! Trust Him, and He will take care of it.

He has had some of the most hopeless cases. He was able to heal all that came to Him while on earth. He is the same today.

. . .We must trust God in time of trouble, in time of bereavement. You can trust Him with your soul until your dying day, if you will. Will you not do it? D. L. MOODY

New Growth in Faithfulness

If I focus all of my attention on the problem, it becomes my god. If I focus my attention on God, He becomes the solution.

Brother Angel

On a hot afternoon in a late August of my childhood, my younger brother Tim and I were bunkered down in the trunk of our brother Steve's car, single-handedly holding off a platoon of Nazi soldiers. The backseat was packed to the roof with college paraphernalia, but since the trunk was empty, it was a good place to make a stand for God, mother, apple pie, and the American Way.

Fighting a war wasn't in our initial plans. Originally, our objective was to ride in the trunk all the way to Steve's Fort Wayne college campus. When he opened his trunk, it would be a fine surprise for him to find his little brother and sister inside. Then we could meet all his friends, see his room, and maybe spend the night in the dorm. But as the afternoon dragged on and Steve and Dad fooled around with a stereo system in the house, our imagination morphed the trunk into a tank and us into a couple of brave World War II Allied soldiers.

Through the edges of the lowered lid, we watched for signs of the approaching enemy, occasionally shooting back at snipers behind the peony bushes. Suddenly, a mortar attack took out the swing set and the cherry tree. Then the enemy launched a mighty offensive.

"The Germans are coming! The Germans are coming!" Tim yelled in warning, and then in a great act of selfless bravery, slammed shut the tank cover that suddenly turned into a securely locked trunk lid. Then all was quiet on the battlefront as realization dawned that the enemy had two prisoners of war that were being held in the trunk of their brother's Pontiac!

In the matter of minutes, the trunk became an airless oven, and we realized that the Nazis would chalk up two more casualties if we didn't get out very soon. Frantically, we tried yelling for help to no avail; no one could hear us over the music. As the heat grew, we soon lay exhausted and breathless in the sticky, dusty darkness. Gasping for air in that morsel of hell, we decided to beg God for help.

Once our prayers were sent up, we lay quietly on our backs, nearly too exhausted and breathless to move. Halfheartedly, we pushed against the lid with our feet, resigned to whatever befell us. Then, suddenly, a beam of light appeared, momentarily blinding us. A burnished-headed man towered over us. For a fleeting second, I thought it was an angel, but as my eyes readjusted to the land of the living, I realized that it was merely Steve looking for a stereo part he thought he'd left in the trunk; however, he looked pretty good to me just then!

A major part of faithfulness is thanksgiving. Far too often, lessons learned and promises made in the foxhole are quickly forgotten. But when God steps out of heaven, rescues us from our own folly, and preserves our lives, we should celebrate the occasion for a lifetime.

Those should be the stories we tell our children, the tales we share with friends. For if we were to be totally honest with ourselves and with others, the hero of every near miss is God, and the retelling of each story is a heaven-sent opportunity for a faithful witness.

Would our lives have been any different if a certified member of the heavenly hosts had rescued us? Probably not, because we knew beyond a doubt that God had sent Steve. Would our eternity be different if we kept the story to ourselves? Maybe not only ours, but the eternity of others as well.

A Faith That Endures Hardship

A number of years ago I knew a woman who found God to be a very wonderful Friend. She had a rich Christian experience, but there came into her life a very great trial: her home was broken up; the crash was unspeakable; in the midst of it all it seemed that her Father forsook her.

One evening after prayer-meeting she arose and gave this testimony. We all knew how precious God was to her. Her face was pale and thin. She had suffered much. "God and I have been such wonderful friends, but He seems very far away. He seems to have withdrawn Himself from me. I seem to be left utterly alone." Then looking off into the distance, and with tears, she continued, "But if I never see His face again, I will keep looking at the spot where I saw His face last."

I have never seen nor heard of anything finer than that. That is mighty, sublime, glorious faith that keeps going on. There is a wonderful outcome to the trials in a life of victorious faith like this. This was Job's greatest triumph: "He knoweth the way that I take. The Lord gave and the Lord hath taken away. Blessed be the Name of the Lord." DEAN DUTTON

When we go through painful times, when the Master Gardener is hard at work in our lives weeding and pruning, sometimes we feel as though our faith falters. After all, we may not be able to feel God's presence in our lives. But faith and feelings are two different things. Feelings come and go—but faith just keeps on looking toward God, no matter how many trials seem to block our view of His face.

Weeding Out Our Lack of Faith
A Prayer

Lord,
Unless I trust You wholly, I am not faithful. Show me where I doubt You. Help my unbelief.

Unless I love my enemies as You have loved me, I am not faithful. Show me my indifference and resentment. Give me supernatural charity to pass along to others.

Unless I do good to those who spitefully use me, I am not faithful. Show me what acts of kindness I should do. Give me the strength to do them.

Unless I am mindful of You, I cannot be faithful. Show me where I shut You out. Help my mind to focus on You.

Dear Lord,
Your compassion and love are new every morn-
ing: Great is Your faithfulness. Help me to be the
child of my Heavenly Father and also be faithful.
In the morning, during the light of day when
everything is fine, let my life show Your loving-
kindness. Let me demonstrate Your faithful

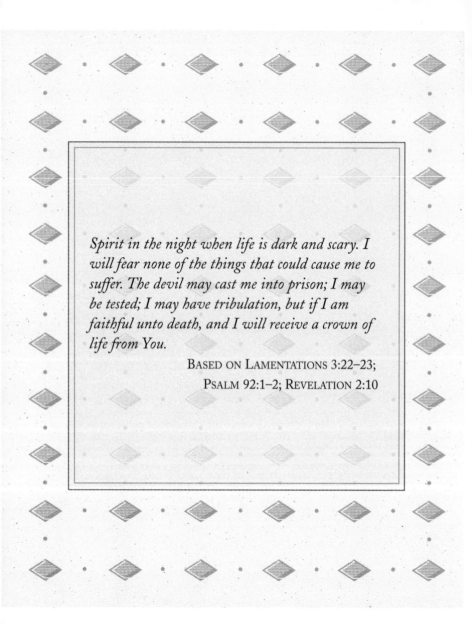

Spirit in the night when life is dark and scary. I will fear none of the things that could cause me to suffer. The devil may cast me into prison; I may be tested; I may have tribulation, but if I am faithful unto death, and I will receive a crown of life from You.

BASED ON LAMENTATIONS 3:22–23;
PSALM 92:1–2; REVELATION 2:10

Chapter 6

Mature Growth

"Consider the lilies of the field, how they grow; they toil not, neither do they spin: And yet I say unto you, that even Solomon in all his glory was not arrayed like one of these. Wherefore, if God so clothe the grass of the field, which to day is, and to morrow is cast in the oven, shall he not much more clothe you, O ye of little faith?"

MATTHEW 6:28–30

Watch ye,

stand fast in the faith. . .be strong.

1 CORINTHIANS 16:13

God does not want our faith to remain a seedling throughout our lives. Instead, He wants us to grow into full maturity, so that our faith will be strong enough to face whatever life brings.

Be steadfast as a tower that doth not bend
Its stately summit to the tempest's shock.
DANTE

Give me. . .

my staff of faith to walk upon. . .

my bottle of salvation,

my gown of glory,

hope's true gage,

and thus I'll take my pilgrimage.

SIR WALTER RALEIGH

Developing Deep Roots
of Faithfulness

Just as in any growing relationship, you must spend time with God in order for faithful love to bud and bear fruit. Try to set aside a certain time each day for this.

Fertilizer Application

Apply prayer and Scripture reading once a day to maintain a minimum level of health; twice a day for moderate development; three times a day for rapid growth.

The prophet Daniel—whose employer was a despotic Eastern king inclined to lopping off heads without much provocation—set aside three times each day to worship God (Daniel 6:10). If you work for someone with a similar disposition, try praising and praying three times a day. God's power is still as great today as it was in Daniel's time.

David recommended in the Psalms that we seek God early and also meditate on His Word morning and night. Make a conscious decision to make a daily date with God—and keep it!

Instructions for Fertilizer Application

Before you begin your time with God, ask the Holy Spirit to reveal to you the meaning of the Bible verses you are going to read. Ask Him to open your eyes and prepare your heart to the messages of the Word.

> *The goal of faithfulness is not that we will do work for God, but that He will be free to do His work through us. God calls us to His service and places tremendous responsibilities on us. He expects no complaining on our part and offers no explanation on His part. God wants to use us as He used His own Son.* OSWALD CHAMBERS

Planting an Eternal Harvest
Disciplines to Grow a Faithful Soul

It requires real dedication for a teenager to get out of bed at 6 A.M., but on any given school day, Suzanne crawled out of her warm blankets to spend time with the Lord. Challenged by her youth club director to have daily devotions, she had decided to make it a habit.

A HARVEST OF FAITHFULNESS

At first, the "thees" and "thous" obscured the meaning of the text in her King James Version Bible, but as she persisted with her studies, she eventually could look past the ancient English to the eternal truths contained in the words. After a while, she used other translations of the Bible as well, but she loved the poetry of the King James Version.

"I was reared in a Christian home, and I had made a commitment to Jesus at a young age. But it wasn't until I began to study the Bible for myself that the Holy Spirit sparked in my heart a passion for God. Before that, I heard about God, but I hadn't experienced Him.

"I came to look forward to my private time with God as the best moments of the day. I derived such strength and growth from those times, that they were more vital to me than food or drink."

Now that Suzanne has become an adult, she has tried to keep alive her personal moments with God, but she hasn't always succeeded. "Sometimes I would just get so tired from my daily responsibilities, it was easier to sleep that extra half hour in the morning or sit down and watch the television at night, instead of spending time with God. But when I did that, eventually I would find myself faintly depressed, anxious, and overeating junk food. I would realize that I hadn't fed my soul and that I was fainting from hunger," said Suzanne. "My spiritual life not only flourishes when I have my quiet time with

God, but my whole day goes better when I begin the day in the throne room of God."

I trust in the same powerful God,
that His holy arm and power
will carry me through,
whatever He hath yet for me to do.
. . . I know His faithfulness
and goodness,
and I have experienced His Love.

MARGARET FELL FOX

Fired by God

Vic discovered that when a person is seeking God's direction, life will sometimes take surprising turns.

A HARVEST OF FAITHFULNESS

On a late spring afternoon in Findlay, Ohio, as he was driving his 1946 Pontiac to the pizza place where he worked, Vic recommitted himself to serving God. "Your will be done with my life," Vic remembers praying, never dreaming that God would take him at his word. Within the next several minutes, God rearranged his entire future.

As a student working his way through college, Vic had been making pizzas for about nine months. While he didn't intend to make a career of it, he had been giving it his best effort. However, on that afternoon, the assistant manager met him at the door to inform him of a change in his employment status.

"You're fired!"

"I was startled," Vic remembers, "but a thrill surged through me as I remembered the commitment I had just made. I was sure this was the hand of God working."

Badly in need of a paycheck, Vic took a job as an orderly at Blanchard Valley Hospital. However, his occupation was about to change again: Because of his college training, in addition to his orderly duties, Vic was sent to the lab to do emergency tests. Over test tubes and microscopes, he became acquainted with the hospital pathologist who needed someone to assist him with autopsies. He tapped Vic for the job. Vic showed such aptitude that he was placed on call for all of the autopsies in the county and the hospital.

Sometime later, Vic decided to apply to medical school. He

knew admissions standards were rigorous. Nervously, he interviewed with the acceptance committee on Friday. When he returned to school on Sunday afternoon, there was a letter in his mailbox. The pathologist with whom Vic worked at the hospital was also on the staff of the Ohio State Medical School. He had given Vic a glowing recommendation that helped cinch his admittance.

"Is getting fired a miracle?" asks Vic.

It is when God is leading. Vic has now been a surgeon for more than twenty-five years and has served as a medical missionary in various parts of the world for more than ten years.

Let us hold fast

the profession of our faith

without wavering;

(for he is faithful).

HEBREWS 10:23

A HARVEST OF FAITHFULNESS

Because we cannot see the hand of God in our affairs, we rush to the conclusion that He has lost sight of them and of us. We look at the "seeming" of things instead of at the underlying facts, and declare that, because God is unseen, He must necessarily be absent. And especially this is the case if we are conscious of having ourselves wandered away from Him and forgotten Him. We judge Him by ourselves, and think that He must also have forgotten and forsaken us. We. . . find it hard to believe He can be faithful when we know ourselves to be so unfaithful.

HANNAH WHITALL SMITH

Growing Strong in the Desert

King David apparently had numerous incidents when he had a great need and only God could supply it. You will find his prayers for God's intervention in the Psalms. Insert your name and situation into David's prayers and see how God will supply your needs as He did David's.

- ◆ When you're surrounded by enemies and feel deserted by God—PSALM 3

- When you're in distress—PSALM 4

- When you're being slandered—PSALMS 5, 70

- When you're weary from your troubles—PSALM 6

- When you're being persecuted—PSALMS 7, 64

- When you're feeling oppressed—PSALMS 10, 54

- When you feel abandoned by God—PSALM 13

- When you need God's preservation—PSALM 16

- When you need God's protection—PSALM 17

- When you need God's wisdom—PSALM 18:18–33

- When you are suffering from depression
  —PSALMS 22, 63

- When you have sinned—PSALMS 25, 51

- When you need God's strength—PSALM 28

A HARVEST OF FAITHFULNESS

- When you feel alone—PSALM 31:7–21

- When you have been lied about—PSALM 35

- When you are ill—PSALM 38

- When you are troubled in spirit—PSALM 42

- When you have enemies—PSALMS 55, 59

- When you need deliverance—PSALM 57

- When you have been wronged—PSALM 69

Prayers for Guidance in Uncertain Times

Dear Lord,
When the Israelites left Egypt and were preparing to cross
the desert, You sent a pillar of cloud to guide them by day
and a pillar of fire to give light in the night so they could
travel either by day or night. Send them for me. (Exodus
13:21–22)

I will trust in You, Lord, with all my heart and not lean on my own understanding. In all my ways, I will acknowledge You, and you will make my paths straight. (Proverbs 3:5–6)

Teach me Your way, Lord. Lead me in a straight path because of my oppressors. (Psalm 27:11)

As I run to the path of Your commands, You will set my heart free. (Psalm 119:32)

I will take Your Word as a lamp to my feet and a light for my path. (Psalm 119:105)

Sometimes we want things we were not meant to have. Because He loves us, the Father says no. Faith trusts that no.

ELISABETH ELLIOT

A HARVEST OF FAITHFULNESS

Enduring Dry Seasons
Mature Faith Is Undaunted

After many prayers, Bill and Carol were able to adopt a newborn boy. "I can't tell you how overjoyed we were!" said Bill.

A pretty, albeit cranky, baby, Bill and Carol assumed little Billy's fussiness was normal. But as the child grew, his moods alternated between charming and explosive. Finally, Carol took Billy to a pediatrician and mental health counselor, both of whom diagnosed him with a condition caused by maternal and perhaps by paternal consumption of alcoholic beverages. Although academically bright, Billy would always have trouble learning from his mistakes or correction. His emotional maturity level would remain that of a six- or seven-year-old child. The counselor warned Bill and Carol that an overwhelming number of adults with this disability end up in the penal system because of their explosiveness and poor judgment.

Bill and Carol would not believe this could be their Billy's fate. After all, they read Bible stories and nightly prayed with him and for him, took him to church, and enrolled him in a Christian school.

Now in junior high, however, Billy was rebellious and inclined toward violent outbursts. Heartbroken, Carol began meeting with several Christian women who fasted and prayed for the lives and souls of their children. "Moses was an adopted child who was rebellious," said Carol. "He even committed murder and had to hide for his life in the wilderness. I'm sure his parents, both his adoptive parents and his biological ones, despaired for his future. Yet God was able to redeem Moses' ruined life.

"Although my son keeps me on my knees, I am not discouraged," said Carol. "Since it is not God's will that any should perish but that all should come to repentance (2 Peter 3:9), when I pray for my son, I 'see' him with the eyes of faith, whole in God. If God can turn Moses' life around on the back side of the desert, He can reach my son."

By faith we understand that the universe was formed at God's command, so that what is seen was not made out of what was visible.

By faith Abel offered God a better sacrifice than Cain did. By faith he was commended as a righteous man, when God spoke well of his offerings. And by faith he still speaks, even though he is dead.

By faith Enoch was taken from this life, so that he did not experience death; he could not be found, because God had taken him away. For before he was taken, he was commended as one who pleased God. And without faith it is impossible to please God. . . .

By faith Noah, when warned about things not yet

seen, in holy fear built an ark to save his family. By his
faith he condemned the world, and became heir of the
righteousness that comes by faith.

By faith Abraham, when called to go to a place he
would later receive as his inheritance, obeyed and went,
even though he did not know where he was going. By faith
he made his home in the promised land like a stranger in a
foreign country. . . . For he was looking forward to the city
with foundations, whose architect and builder is God.

By faith Abraham, even though he was past age—
and Sarah herself was barren—was enabled to become a
father because he considered him faithful who had made
the promise. . . .

All these people were still living by faith when they
died. They did not receive the things promised; they only
saw them and welcomed them from a distance.

HEBREWS 11:3–11, 13 NIV

Testing—The Growing Season of Faithfulness

Satan taunted God concerning Job's unmistakable faithfulness: "Does Job fear God for nothing? Have You not put a

hedge around him and his household and everything he has? . . .But stretch out your hand and strike everything he has, and he will surely curse you to your face" (Job 1:9, 11 NIV).

As Satan pointed out, faithfulness to God is easy when everything is going our way. But our faithfulness is put to the test when troubles come our way. In those circumstances, the Scriptures give us precise instructions on how to handle problems:

> *My brethren, count it all joy when ye fall into divers temptations; knowing this, that the trying of your faith worketh patience. But let patience have her perfect work, that ye may be perfect and entire, wanting nothing. If any of you lack wisdom, let him ask of God, that giveth to all men liberally, and upbraideth not; and it shall be given him.*
>
> JAMES 1:2–5

"Why?" is not the question one should ask God when in a troubling situation. The question is "What?" "What 'perfect work' are You trying to refine in me?" and "What do You want me to do with this mess?"

Then rejoice—count the problem a joy—because God is going to do something miraculous in you!

A HARVEST OF FAITHFULNESS

*We have the idea that God rewards us for our faith, and
it may be so in the initial stages. But we do not earn anything through faith—faith brings us into the right relationship with God and gives Him His opportunity to
work. Yet God frequently has to knock the bottom out of
your experience as His saint to get you in direct contact
with Himself. God wants you to understand that it is a
life of faith, not a life of emotional enjoyment of His
blessings. The beginning of your life of faith was very
narrow and intense, centered around a small amount of
experience that had as much emotion as faith in it, and
it was full of light and sweetness. Then God withdrew
His conscious blessings to teach you to "walk by faith"
(2 Corinthians 5:7).*   OSWALD CHAMBERS

Mature Faith in the Face of Fear

Screaming brakes. Grinding metal. Breaking glass. "Joel!"

Bekah's eyes snapped open into the darkness of her bed-
room. Another nightmare! Although she knew—or thought
she knew—that her eighteen-year-old son was asleep in the
next room, she jumped out of bed and went into his room to

make sure he was still there and breathing. She found him balled up in his covers, sleeping in the same position he had slept in as a toddler. Back in her room, Bekah crawled into bed, drenched with sweat but chilled to the bone with terror.

She had had this dream many times before, and she wasn't sure exactly what it meant or what she was supposed to do with her fear. In the dream, Joel was always in a car accident and each time he was either killed or paralyzed. The dream had become increasingly frequent.

"I would just lay in bed and pray. Sometimes, I would pray for Joel's safety from all harm. Other times, I would just beg God to at least spare the life of my son," said Bekah.

Bekah had already buried one child. She and her husband had lost a son almost sixteen years earlier, and she never wanted to experience that pain again. But as the dream became more frequent, Bekah knew she was going to have to do something. She couldn't live her life haunted by fear.

"Lord, what is the meaning of this dream? What do You want me to do about it?" she asked God.

Pray for Joel's safety, seemed to be the reply. *Trust Me.*

So she decided that each time the dream came, she would get on her knees and pray for Joel's safety. And she did.

Meanwhile, Joel's little subcompact car had one mechanical problem after another, and he was occasionally forced to drive his dad's pride and joy, a near-mint-condition 1973

Cadillac El Dorado. "That Caddy was huge!" said Bekah. "It was like trying to drive the Queen Mary down the road."

On a Saturday morning, the sixteenth anniversary of her older son's death, Joel's car once again balked in the garage. He told Bekah that he was taking the Cadillac to drive to work.

"He kissed me good-bye and left. When I heard the sirens go off up the street at the police station not ten minutes later, I watched the ambulance and emergency personnel fly down the street, never once dreaming they were heading to help my son," said Bekah. But a few minutes later, a neighbor pounded on her door.

"Joel's been in an accident!" he told her. "I'll take you there."

"When we pulled up," Bekah remembered, "the scene was exactly like I had seen it in my dreams. The front of Joel's car was crunched up and broken glass was everywhere. A van full of kids was in the ditch, and the emergency workers were trying to get the kids on stretchers. The ambulance carrying Joel was already heading for the hospital, and I had to restrain myself from chasing it down the highway."

Joel's injuries were serious, but not life-threatening, though his recovery was long and slow. "The accident was in no way Joel's fault. It could have been so much worse," said Bekah. "There were a dozen details that had they been different, Joel could have been paralyzed or killed. For example, if he had been driving his own car, he probably would have been killed.

But that big Caddy protected him.

"I believe God, who knows the future, sent those dreams, not so I would worry, but so I would pray for Joel's safety. With all the praying I'd been doing, I'm certain the angels were all at their battle stations by the time the accident occurred."

Way To Grow!

A person would have to be a fool not to recognize troubles when they appear on the horizon. This is the difference between a mature Christian and a person still full of doubt: The person whose faith has grown strong sees a looming problem as an opportunity for God to show His care and demonstrate His miraculous power.

But all of us still have those sleepless nights when problems cast tall shadows on the wall. How should a faithful believer turn the bane of worry into the blessing of assurance? Here are some suggestions:

- Focus on the promises of God instead of the worry. Some promises that will encourage you are:

Cast your cares on the LORD

and he will sustain you;

he will never let the righteous fall.

PSALM 55:22 NIV

Be careful for nothing: but in every thing, by prayer and supplication with thanksgiving let your requests be made known unto God. And the peace of God, which passeth all understanding, shall keep your hearts and minds through Christ Jesus. PHILIPPIANS 4:6–7

Humble yourselves therefore under the mighty hand of God, that he may exalt you in due time: casting all your care upon him: for he careth for you. 1 PETER 5:6–7

♦ Ask God how you should pray. Is He trying to get you moving? Does He want you to stay on your knees and fight a spiritual battle? Ask God for wisdom so you can pray in His will, then stay on your knees until you feel a release in your spirit that your prayers have been answered.

- Present your worry before the throne and leave it there. Picture yourself placing your concerns into the nail-scarred, capable hands of Jesus.

- Thank God before you receive the answer. God will answer your prayers for help. A faithful heart doesn't have to wait to see the answers with physical eyes to be thankful. A faithful heart will thank Him in advance.

The Courage to be Faithful

On a clear summer day, my family and I walked along an abandoned railroad track through the countryside. Little sulfur yellow butterflies flickered over the tall weeds. Red-winged blackbirds called out to one another as we walked through their territories.

The children were busy picking up colored rocks and rusty artifacts left behind by the iron horse that had once rumbled through the farmlands. There was so much for them to see that they were running and exploring everywhere, while our old dog tried to keep up. My oldest son stooped to pick up an old piece of board that looked interesting to him. He was stopped still

A HARVEST OF FAITHFULNESS

by a frightened squeak.

Beneath the board was a mouse nest. Mama mouse was lying on her side, with several baby mice nursing. She looked up at the giant boy and dog, and her eyes popped wide with fear. She rose up on one tiny foot as if she was going to dash away, but then she lay back down again with her babies. They were too small to run, and she wasn't going anywhere without them. She was helpless to protect them, but she wasn't going to abandon them, either, so she bared her teeth in the most ferocious look that two inches of rodent could muster.

For a moment frozen in time and memory, both boy and dog stared, fascinated with the mice. Before I had a chance to utter, "Don't touch her!" my son carefully set the board roof down over the mouse family and pulled the dog away.

Over the years, we've talked about the mother mouse and her little family. What courage the little mouse had in the face of threatened destruction! Some days, we need that same courage to be faithful.

Allowing Our Faith to Mature
Dollars and Sense

Beth said that throughout her life, God has taught her the principle of dollars and sense. "I remember some very tight times in my life when my back was to the wall, and I wondered how God could possibly work out our budget, but every time He has. Sometimes in ways I would never imagine. But the key is to tithe. It makes good cents and good sense to tithe. God has promised to bless us when we do."

One of the most frightening times in Beth's life came when she was putting her husband through college. "We were always short on money, and when I compared our combined wages with our expenses, there was no possible way to make ends meet. But we agreed that we would always tithe. So many times, I would lay our bills on the bed and get on my face before the Lord. 'You multiplied the loaves and fishes,' I'd tell Him. 'You're going to have to multiply the dollars and cents.' And miraculously, He always did. Sometimes, unexpected money would come in the mail. Once we found a $100 bill on the ground. But usually, God just helped us make our strained little budget work. Most of the time, I can't even tell you how.

"I suppose the disciples felt that way, too. They stood right beside Jesus and watched Him feed five thousand men with five loaves and two fishes and they probably couldn't tell you how He did—only that He did! That's the way it is in my life.

I don't know how God helps us make ends meet. I only know He does."

God's blessings are not always monetary. In fact, He blesses us most richly in ways that have nothing to do with our budgets. He helps us "make ends meet" not only financially but also emotionally and spiritually. Open your heart to the Holy Spirit. Say "yes" to His presence in your life. When you do, He will bring you into a faith that's mature and strong, able to withstand whatever life brings.

Father,
Sometimes I am tempted to ask "why?"—but I know that the answer is beyond me. You could tell me, but I probably wouldn't understand any more than I would quantum physics. After I am in Heaven a while, maybe I'll understand both "why" and quantum physics.

In the meantime, tell me "what"—what I should do with this situation—what can I do to get with Your program— and also what I shouldn't do. I don't want to run ahead, but I don't want to lag behind. I want to work with You; I don't want to step on what You're doing and ruin anything. I want to be part of the solution instead of just staring at the problem.

I'm on my knees here, Lord, asking for wisdom. Thank You for never failing me.

Dear Lord,

Examine me, O Lord, and purify me. Try the reins of my heart. I want to be Your servant and Yours alone. I can't serve myself and You. I will worship You and serve You alone. Help me to behave wisely, following in Your perfect way. Even in my most private spaces, help me to walk before You with a perfect heart. I will set no wicked thing before mine eyes. Help

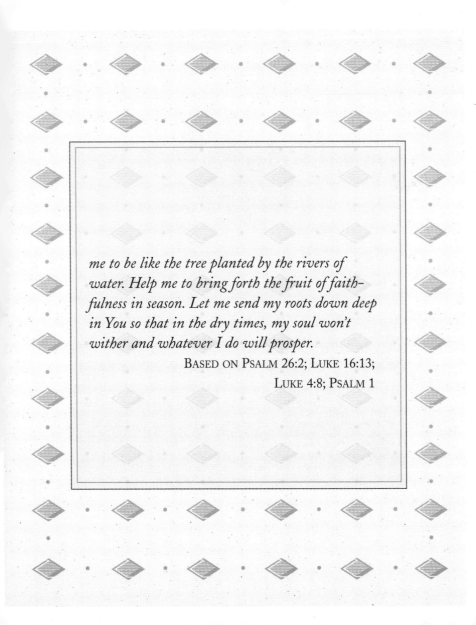

me to be like the tree planted by the rivers of water. Help me to bring forth the fruit of faithfulness in season. Let me send my roots down deep in You so that in the dry times, my soul won't wither and whatever I do will prosper.

BASED ON PSALM 26:2; LUKE 16:13;

LUKE 4:8; PSALM 1

Chapter 7

Shading Others with Our Branches

His branches shall spread, and his beauty shall be as the olive tree, and his smell as Lebanon. They that dwell under his shadow shall. . .revive as the corn, and grow as the vine. HOSEA 14:6–7

Our faith is not merely a private matter, meant for our own souls, something to enjoy in spiritual privacy. No, God wants our faith to benefit those around us. Like a vine that grows tall with thick, luxuriant leaves, our faith should provide shelter and shade, hope and strength to everyone we meet.

May every soul that touches mine—
Be it the slightest contact—
Get therefrom some good;
Some little grace; one kindly thought;
One aspiration yet unfelt;
One bit of courage
For the darkening sky;
One gleam of faith
To brave the thickening ills of life;
One glimpse of brighter skies
Beyond the gathering mists—⸮
To make this life worthwhile. . . .

GEORGE ELIOT

Faithfully Growing in the Image of Christ
Ruth and the Duck

Have you ever piously prayed, "Lord, make me more Christ-like"—and then were shocked when your good intentions were terribly misunderstood by those around you? Don't worry. That might have been the answer to your prayer!

My sister Ruth has a tender heart toward all living creatures

—with the possible exception of bugs. When she lived in southern Florida, she often fed the ducks that swam the canals crisscrossing her neighborhood, and she tried to protect them during hurricanes.

One afternoon while she was running errands, an airborne duck collided with the grill of her husband's new Mercedes. With a sick thud, crackling metal, and screeching brakes, she ground to a halt and leaped out of the car. The grill was shattered, but that was of less concern to her than the unconscious duck. It lay still, bleeding, its pulse pounding in its neck. *Perhaps,* she thought, *if I could get it to the veterinarian, its life might be able to be saved.*

Tenderly, she laid the duck on the floor mat of the front passenger side of the Mercedes and began to frantically maneuver through heavy Florida traffic. A typical afternoon thunderstorm raged overhead as she pulled onto a highway clogged with bumper-to-bumper traffic. Temporarily distracted by the weather and kamikaze drivers, she forgot about the duck for a few moments as lightning flashed, a blinding downpour ensued, and the drivers around her tempted eternity.

Suddenly, the duck shook its head. It blinked several times as if awakening from a bad dream. Then, finding himself in a strange place with his wings still functional, he decided to resume his interrupted flight. Quacking indignantly, he rose up, flew to the back window and hit it with a crack. Dazed but still on wing, he made a 180-degree turn and headed for the windshield. This, too, proved to be a futile and frustrating trip. Increasingly agitated, shedding feathers, bleeding, and lacking any sense of proper toilet manners, the duck circled the interior of the car, occasionally chastising Ruth with beak and wing for putting him in such an undignified circumstance.

Ruth was frantic, too. Not only was she simultaneously being flogged by a duck and threatened by collision, she was going to have to explain to her husband why the grill of his new car was shattered and its interior was decorated with blood, droppings, and feathers. Even to her, the truth had an incredible ring!

The next highway exit provided escape. She pulled over and opened the door. The indignant duck flounced forth without a backward glance at his would-be rescuer, leaving Ruth to contemplate the comparative merits of a hard heart.

Like my sister, we too are often tempted by a bad experience or two to turn a blind eye and deaf ear to the needs around us. We can decide we simply don't want to get involved with the wounded because we recognize there may be a high price to be paid for our efforts. And, like Ruth, we may receive little or no gratitude.

But if we want to become more like Christ, we will direct our hearts to still respond faithfully, to still serve, and to still give. Like Jesus, we may be crucified for our giving—but that will only make us more like Him. Perhaps more like Him than we originally hoped!

The Faithful Use of Our Abilities

At the opening service of the national YMCA convention in Indianapolis, Indiana, a young Civil War veteran and federal tax collector, Ira Sankey, sat listening to the song leader mournfully conduct the singing. Sankey's companion, well aware of Sankey's musical abilities, whispered, "I wish you would start something up there."

So Sankey did. When the song died a natural death on the lips of the singers, Sankey walked to the front and sang a song that so transfixed the assembled men that when the service concluded, D. L. Moody buttonholed Sankey: "Where are you from? What business are you in?" he demanded. When Sankey told him, Moody replied, "You'll have to give that up; I have been looking for you for eight years!"

Sankey was startled, but he promised to make Moody's demand a matter of prayer. He later reported, "I presume I prayed one way and he prayed another; it took him only six months to pray me out of business." Ira Sankey left his secure job collecting money for the United States government to amass souls for the kingdom of Heaven.

Huge crowds flocked to hear Sankey's music and Moody's preaching. Sankey's style was sweet, simple, unaffected, and perfectly attuned to the audience of his day. He sang the words in such a fashion that "souls are receiving Jesus between one note and the next," said an eyewitness.

A natural songwriter, Sankey eventually published six best-selling editions. This netted him a considerable fortune, but he donated all the proceeds to the Dwight L. Moody missionary training school in Northfield, Massachusetts.

If God gives a person great talents, He expects great service from that person. We demonstrate our faithfulness by using our talents for others in the kingdom.

Find the thing meant for you to do and do the best you can. You must be faithful to the place where God put you and for which you are equipped.

HENRY DAVID THOREAU

A Parable of Faithfulness

Jesus gave us a parable about a king who was going to a far country. He called his servants to him. He gave one servant ten talents. To another, he gave five. To yet another, he gave one.

When he returned, he asked the servants to give an accounting of what they had done. The servant given ten talents had earned ten more. The servant with five had earned an additional five.

But the servant with one talent had done nothing with his but bury it in the ground. To keep it safe, he told the king; but the king immediately recognized his actions as unfaithful, wasteful, and lazy. The king rebuked him and threw him out of his kingdom, while the faithful servants were rewarded and commended by the king.

In the Bible's language, a talent was a unit of money, but the meaning of the parable is still clear: God expects you to faithfully use the gifts He has given you. If He has given you ten talents, use them. If He has given you five, use them. And if He has given you only one talent, you better be sure you are using it!

God does not ask us to do anything He has not equipped us to do. Our talents and gifts will always be equal to the job. All we need to do is be faithful to Him with what He's given us.

"Who then is the faithful and wise servant, whom the master has put in charge of the servants in his household. . . ? It will be good for that servant whose master finds him doing so when he returns. I tell you the truth, he will put him in charge of all his possessions."

MATTHEW 24:45–47 NIV

Have you received a ministry from the Lord? If so, you must be faithful to it—to consider your life valuable only for the purpose of fulfilling that ministry. Knowing that you have done what Jesus sent you to do, think how satisfying it will be to hear Him say to you, "Well done, good and faithful servant" (Matthew 25:21 NKJV). *We each have to find a niche in life, and spiritually we find it when we receive a ministry from the Lord. To do this we must have close fellowship with Jesus and must know Him as more than our personal Savior. And we must be willing to experience the full impact of Acts 9:16—"I will show him how many things he must suffer for My name's sake"* (NKJV).

"Do you love Me?" Then, "Feed My sheep" (John 21:17 NKJV). *He is not offering us a choice of how we can serve Him; He is asking for absolute loyalty to His commission, a faithfulness to what we discern when we*

are in the closest possible fellowship with God. If you have received a ministry from the Lord Jesus, you will know that the need is not the same as the call—the need is the opportunity to exercise the call. The call is to be faithful to the ministry you received when you were in true fellowship with Him. This does not imply that there is a whole series of differing ministries marked out for you. It does mean that you must be sensitive to what God has called you to do, and this may sometimes require ignoring demands for service in other areas.

OSWALD CHAMBERS
My Utmost for His Highest

You Were My Faithful Friend

When I was new at church, you were friendly to me. You helped my kids and me find our Sunday school class. You introduced me to your friends. You invited me out to coffee, just to get to know me better. You made me feel at home. You showed me Jesus by being a friend "who sticks closer than a brother."

When I was lonely, you called me on the phone just to say "Hi!" You stopped by the house with freshly baked muffins.

A HARVEST OF FAITHFULNESS

You sent me a kind note. You came and sang carols on my front porch. You invited me to an impromptu get-together at your house. You showed me Jesus by your friendship.

When I was having a busy week, you said, "Let me help." I was too embarrassed to tell you what you could do, but you said, "Just order me around. I'm your servant for the day." You ran errands, dressed the kids, cleaned the bathrooms, frosted cupcakes, and showed me Jesus by your friendship.

When there was a death in my family, you let me cry. You let me talk about my loved one. You let me remember. You didn't try to force me to feel better. You brought food to the house, let my relatives be guests at your house, washed and returned dishes, and showed Jesus to me by your friendship.

When my child was wayward, you didn't condemn. You prayed with me.

When I was unemployed, you brought me job leads. You prayed with me.

When I sinned, you gently corrected me with love. When I hurt you, you forgave me. When I was wrong, you showed me right.

You were faithful. You showed me Jesus.

Faithfulness in Action
To the Faithful Sunday School Teacher
(Dedicated with thanks to Audrey. You know who you are.)

When we giggled about anything and nothing, you laughed with us.

When we put a frog in your purse, you named him "Fred" and added his name to the attendance sheet as a visitor.

When we stumbled over impossible names like "Sheshbazzar" and "Apharsachites," you said, "Substitiute Shes and Aphar," so we could get through the verses without losing the meaning or feeling stupid.

When we were too shy to read aloud from the Bible, you recognized that some kids have "the gift of helps" and found us other jobs so we could still be a part of the class.

When we were young and very wiggly, you put lots of action and fun into the lessons.

You fed us animal crackers to tell the story of Noah's Ark, mixed peanut butter candy to demonstrate the children of Israel making bricks in Egypt (pretzels were the straw), and always gave us a snack because you knew that church could be very, very long after an hour or so in Sunday school.

When we struggled to learn our Bible verses, you made a game out of memorization.

You bribed us with $5 to learn the books of the Old Testament and another $5 if we learned the books of the New

Testament. We remember them to this day.

When we were thirteen years old, rude, and found everything "so boring," you didn't quit in disgust. You stuck with us until we got some sense.

When we got in trouble with the law, you came with us to court.

When we were in the hospital, you visited and sneaked us in a hamburger and French fries.

When our parents wouldn't take us to church, you came early to our house, washed and dressed us, fed us breakfast, took us to Sunday school, sat with us during church, bought us lunch afterward, and took us home.

When we graduated from high school, you helped us figure out what we should do with ourselves.

You prayed we would find jobs.

When we went to college, you sent us encouraging notes and care packages.

You bought us little gifts at Easter and Christmas with your own money.

When our own parents kicked us out of the house, you took us in.

You studied. You planned. You prayed. You cared.

You didn't just teach us about Jesus. You were Jesus.

Is there someone in your life who needs you to be Jesus?

Even prisons and sickrooms
have their special revelations.
It is enough to ask of each of us
that he should be faithful to
his own opportunities and
make the most of
his own blessings.

WILLIAM JAMES

The Welcome Shade of Others' Love

"I was starting to be like Job doing stand-up comedy," a woman pastor said. "So many things had or were going wrong in my life that if I didn't laugh about it, I'd cry and never stop.

"Actually, there was nothing funny about any of it, but frankly, I didn't trust very many people with my pain, so I tried to laugh it off. Also, somewhere I got the idea that it wasn't spiritual to be in as much pain as I was. I couldn't let my parishioners know how much I was really suffering. So I made jokes about the awful things that were happening in my life. When people asked, 'How are you doing?' I'd smile and joke, and they'd assume I was fine.

"Truthfully, I was on the verge of suicide."

The pastor described how she carefully planned her "accident." "It was to be in August on the same day as my birthday, so my family would only have one date to mourn. I bought all of the school clothes for my children, updated my will, paid all the bills, winterized the house, and took a little minivacation at a spot with a notoriously strong offshore current. I'm not a strong swimmer, so it would have been a believable accident."

But God intervened that day in a miraculous fashion. As she was swimming out into the current, someone swam up to her and asked her what she thought she was doing.

"In that moment, all my carefully laid plans just flew away! I couldn't make it look like an accident anymore!" She sat on the beach for a long time, praying for guidance.

"Suddenly, the Lord said to me, 'I'm going to send you a friend.' I told Him, 'I don't want one!' But He knew what I needed."

Her friend came from an unlikely place: from within the pastor's own congregation. "She wasn't necessarily a person I would have picked because she seemed to have a lot of turmoil in her life. I didn't want to burden her with mine, too. But she was nonjudgmental. And she was clever, too. Usually, when someone asked me about myself, I would turn the conversation around to them, and they'd yak on and on and forget about me. She saw through my ploy almost immediately and rarely let me get away with it.

"The other thing I appreciated was that she would pray for me. Sometimes when I asked other people to pray about a situation, I was fairly certain they would forget all about my request as soon as I was out of sight. But if I asked this woman to pray, she'd say, 'Let's pray right now!' She'd put her arm around me then and there and storm the gates of Heaven on my behalf. Although I had been a Christian for years, I think she is the first person I ever allowed to be a true sister in Christ to me. Because of her faithfulness to me, God was able to heal my life."

Be a Faithful Brother or Sister in Christ

We need each other, you and I. We are meant to be friends and family, because we have all been adopted into the family of God through Christ Jesus—so it doesn't matter if we have other things in common or not.

I am a companion of
all them that fear thee,
and of them that keep
thy precepts.

PSALM 119:63

As Christ's followers we are not permitted to congregate into little cliques based on income, personal interests, or any earthly category. Instead, we should automatically consider anyone of the household of faith to be our brother or sister in Christ. We love and cherish them; we don't slander them, nor do we permit others to be unkind to them. They're family.

"We had a mentally retarded young man at our church who genuinely loved the Lord," said Leslie, "but he was inclined to doing some socially inappropriate things now and then, like picking his nose in public or scratching himself whenever and wherever he happened to itch. Some people in the church thought it reflected badly on our particular congregation to have such a person as a member. But really, he was one of 'the least of these' that Jesus was talking about in Matthew 25:45. If we were kind to this man, then we were being kind to Jesus—and if we rejected him, then we were rejecting Jesus as well."

Servant of All

Faithful friendship means we are meant to serve each other. It is a great honor to serve our fellow brothers and sisters in Christ. Read these words of Jesus based on Matthew 20:25–28:

> *Whoever wants to become great among you must be your servant, and whoever wants to be first must be your slave—just as the Son of Man did not come to be served, but to serve, and to give his life as a ransom for many.*

Surprise! I'm a Gift to You!

Faithful friendship means we are gifts to one another. In other words, you use your God-given talents to benefit me; I use mine to benefit you. Together, by mutually giving ourselves to one another, we glorify Christ.

> *There is something vital, energetic, active, mighty about this kind of faith! It is impossible for it not to be engaged in good works without ceasing. Nor does it ask whether good works are to be done, but before one asks, faith has already spontaneously done them, and goes on doing them continuously.*
>
> *. . .In consequence, a man of faith becomes willing and anxious, without any prompting, to do good to all men, to serve the common good, to suffer all things for the love and praise of God, who has shown him such grace.*
>
> *It will now be seen how it is impossible to separate works from faith, as impossible as it is to separate burning and shining from fire.* MARTIN LUTHER

Faithful Service
Cary and the Big Underpants

As a children's pastor in a medium-sized church, I tried to prepare my young congregation for the thunderclap of adolescence with a discipling class. Of course we discussed private devotions and prayer, but because preteens are notoriously self-absorbed, I emphasized service to others. A trip to a local nursing home was to be the apex of this section of our class.

I was a little nervous about the trip. Introducing the kinetic energy of preadolescents into the overheated, camphor-laden atmosphere of the nursing home was like mixing nitro and glycerin. Something explosive was bound to happen!

One of the boys, Cary, was a quiet introvert. He was a sad child with trouble in his home. I suspected his presence on the outing wasn't voluntary; his parents had probably forced him to go with the class to the nursing home.

Once inside, most of the other kids went gaily off to collect the residents and push their chairs into the activity room, occasionally startling the elderly patients by popping "wheelies" with the chairs. But Cary hung behind. He was visibly uncomfortable, but because I believe that labor is good for whatever ails a person, I put him to work searching for hymnals.

He halfheartedly poked around inside a bookcase and came up empty-handed. But when he opened the piano bench, he hit pay dirt—and more. There were the hymnbooks, all right, but on top of them was what looked like a rag. Without thinking, Cary held it up—and discovered it wasn't a rag at all but a gigantic and very wet pair of underpants. One of the elderly women, no doubt embarrassed and ashamed, had tucked them there where they'd be out of sight.

My heart sank. Poor Cary! I knew he wasn't very happy to be at the nursing home in the first place, and now this. I wondered if he'd bolt for the hills and we'd never see him again.

Our eyes met over the pants. I couldn't help but smile. Suddenly, he grinned. "I found the hymnbooks." He lifted the hymnbooks, put the panties back in the bench, and quietly shut it.

The activity room soon filled with our congregation and the exuberant preteens. The service went forward without a hitch. Afterwards, we discussed the visit. All of the kids, even Cary, said that they enjoyed the trip.

"I think I got more out of it than I gave," Cary muttered, his face a little pink. That, of course, is the way all service to others turns out—especially when we do it for God as well.

As Christmas of 1955 approached, Pastor Carl couldn't help but notice the dilapidated old houses that straggled along the hilly Sangamon River road that lead through his parish in West Decatur, Illinois. He knew well that those houses sheltered very poor families and hungry children.

Carl and his wife had financial pressures of their own—and eight children, too, ranging in age from two to sixteen. However, recalling God's promise, He that has pity upon the poor lends to the Lord; and that which he has given will He pay him again (Proverbs 19:17), Carl filled a bushel-sized fruit basket with groceries, including a ham, and delivered it to the family in one of the shabbiest homes. Carl felt a little nervous about how his own family was going to be fed that Christmas, but he had decided to trust that detail to God. "When I returned home," Carl remembers, "sitting on our porch was an almost identical basket of groceries, including a ham. God had kept His word."

The following Christmas, Carl and his family had relocated to a different parish several states away. Although family finances were again tight, Carl once more filled a basket with groceries and a ham. He gave the basket to a family experiencing hard times.

After making the delivery, he stopped at the bank. One of

the tellers handed him something and said, "I want to give this to you."

In Carl's hand was a check for $25—just the cost of the basket of groceries.

When we are faithful to others, we can count on God to be faithful to us.

Faithfulness at Home

Others will see our faithfulness at church, at work, in our community—but more than anywhere else, we live out our faithfulness in our homes. In the midst of our families' intimate needs, we spread the branches of our faith, offering shade and shelter to those we love the most.

A Faithful Mother's Prayer

The first moment she knew that there was new life within her, she prayed, "Dear God, Create this child's inmost being and knit him together properly. All his days are written in Your book" (see Psalm 139:13–16).

When the pains of labor came upon her, she prayed, "Although my child now walks through the valley of the shadow of death, I will fear no evil, for You are with him" (see Psalm 23:4).

When she first held her baby in her arms, she prayed, "Like a loving Shepherd, gather this little lamb in Your arms, and carry him in Your bosom" (see Isaiah 40:11).

When she presented him to the Lord, she prayed, "Draw this child to Yourself from his earliest days. Take him in Your hands and bless him, for of such is the kingdom of heaven" (see Matthew 19:14).

When he was in his "terrible twos," she prayed, "Help me train up this child in the way he should go, so that when he is old, he will not depart from it" (see Proverbs 22:6).

When her child started school, she prayed, "Don't let my son forget Your laws, but let his heart keep Your commandments. I know they will give him length of days, long life, and peace" (see Proverbs 3:1–2).

When she and her child ran errands, she prayed, "Help me to diligently teach Your words to my child, and talk of them when we are sitting in our house and when we walk by the way, and when we lie down and when we rise up" (see Deuteronomy 6:7).

When she washed and folded her child's clothes, she

prayed, "Clothe my child in the Lord Jesus Christ, and do not let him gratify the desires of his sinful nature" (see Romans 13:14).

When she had to correct her child, she prayed, "Help me to chasten my child and drive foolishness far from him. Let me bring him up nurtured and admonished by the Lord" (see Proverbs 19:18; 22:15; Ephesians 6:4).

When her son grew into a teenager, she prayed, "Help him to remember his Creator in the days of his youth" (see Ecclesiastes 12:1).

When her son was rebellious, she prayed, "Teach my child to walk in the ways of the Lord and to know that rebellion brings sorrow" (see Ecclesiastes 11:9–10).

When her son was interested in girls, she prayed, "Help him to flee youthful lusts but follow righteousness, faith, charity, peace with them that call on the Lord out of a pure heart" (see 2 Timothy 2:22).

When her son was choosing a career, the mother prayed, "Lord, be with my child and prosper him; help him to build a house of the Lord. Give him wisdom and understanding that he may keep Your law" (see 1 Chronicles 22:11–12).

When her son chose a mate, she prayed, "Help my child to leave us and cleave to his mate, so that the two become one flesh" (see Genesis 2:24).

When her son made her a grandmother, she prayed, "Let

my son and his wife observe and hear all of Your words, that it may go well with them, and their children after them forever" (see Deuteronomy 12:28).

The Long-Term Results of Faithfulness

"Grandpa George died long before I was born," writes a middle-aged woman, "but his commitment to Christ has had a major impact on my life."

She was writing about her grandfather, an orphaned son of a Civil War veteran who was reared in a series of abusive foster homes. His growth stunted by starvation, his feet deformed from frostbite and from wearing cast-off shoes several sizes too small, he had been overworked, horsewhipped for trifles, and denied an education. As the 1800s waned, life looked bleak for this young man. Then, at twelve years of age, he was placed in the home of a childless, elderly couple: the Skinners. These people were different from any he had ever known; they were devout Christians who took young George under their wing and loved him in Christ. Under their kind tutelage, he learned to read, write, and serve Jesus. He never forgot what they taught him.

When he sought a wife, he looked for a woman who loved

Christ with the same passion as himself. Suspecting that he had found her, on December 13, 1896, he wrote in her autograph book:

> *We ourselves shape the joy and fears*
> *Of which the life to come is made.*
> *And fill our future atmosphere*
> *With sunshine or with shade.*

He married his sweetheart, reared a large family, and loved Jesus. A spectacular farmer, he remained faithful to Christ his entire life.

"As much as we can ascertain, none of Grandfather George's forebears were Christians. Nor were any of his siblings. But he began a heritage that continues in his family to this day," said his granddaughter. "He demonstrated an example of godliness to my father, who in turn showed it to me. So although he died before I was born, Grandfather George has indeed shaped my life. Because of his faithful commitment to Christ, the atmosphere of my life was filled with sunshine—and Sonshine."

Propagating by Root Cuttings—
Begin the Tradition

You may come from a family tree whose roots have long been planted in Jesus. Or you may be a first-generation Christian. Whichever the case may be, you can pass along the stories of your family's adventures in faith to your children and grand-children. They will enjoy the stories, and they will help cement in their hearts the vow made by Joshua: "As for me and my house, we will serve the LORD" (Joshua 24:15).

Here are some fun family activities for commemorating faithfulness:

- Tell your story. Do your children know how you accepted Christ to be your Lord? Share your story, then take turns telling each individual's faith history, allowing even the youngest to participate.

- One night a week at the supper table or during family devotions, tell about a time God answered a prayer for you.

- Keep a family journal of prayer requests and praises. Refer to it often to update answered prayers.

- Start holiday traditions that promote faithfulness to Christian principles. Instead of a Halloween party, have your kids dress as Bible characters, keeping their "identities" secret. Play "Twenty Questions" to discover who they are.

- While many people plan their Christmas menus and decorations, you may want to plan how your family is going to celebrate Christ on His birthday.

- Encourage your children to tithe from their allowance and earnings. When they are young, begin what will hopefully become a lifelong habit by giving each child a "tithe jar," or a special bank to hold offering money until Sunday services. Make tithing a joyful occasion, not a big imposition. Celebrate that you can give back some money to Jesus.

A Faithful Servant
of a Faithful God

He was so young and so far, far away from home. No one ever need know except the two of them—and God, of course, but maybe He would overlook it.

This woman understood him better than anyone had for a very long time because she, too, was terribly lonely. Her soldier husband was always gone, and when he was home, he was too busy climbing the ladder of success to pay much attention to her. What was wrong with giving her a little solace while taking some for himself? After all, they were both adults.

God knew that so many other things in his life had been bad. His family life had consisted of one conflict after another. His mother died when he was just a tyke, his father had been a single parent, and there was trouble with the blended family and his half brothers. Why, those half brothers of his had literally sold him down the river! Didn't he have the right to grab a little happiness wherever he could find it?

She was beautiful and she wanted him. She had made that clear in little ways almost from the first. She sought him out to ask questions, watched him carefully, and subtly promoted his career with her husband, Potiphar, who was also his employer. Because Potiphar was gone on the king's business so much, he relied heavily on her recommendations, and she liked what she saw of Joseph. Potiphar agreed with her. One day, he handed Joseph his bankbook and the house keys and said, "Everything I have is in your hands, except my wife, of course!" They all laughed except Mrs. Potiphar, who smiled and winked at Joseph.

From then on, the pressure went from subtle to intense.

Joseph firmly ignored her hints, so she made her advances less and less oblique until she was flatly demanding, "Come to bed with me!"

There were more excuses why he should sleep with her than reasons why he shouldn't. In the end, there was only one compelling reason why he should resist her advances: It was wrong. It would be an offense to God.

Was there any reason he should care what God thought? God was so far away and Mrs. Potiphar was right in from of him, right now. She could help his career a great deal and, generally speaking, slaves didn't have much of a future. Refusing her advances could even put him at peril of his life. Was faithfulness to a distant God worth losing his life?

The moment of truth eventually came. One day, it was just the two of them, Joseph and Mrs. Potiphar, all alone in the house. No one was expected home for quite a while; no one would ever know.

She quietly approached him from behind, gently touching his muscular shoulders. "Joseph!" she said. He turned and she caught him in her arms.

She squeezed her body against his. "Now, Joseph! This is our time!"

Somewhere, somehow, Joseph had counted the cost and decided faithfulness to God was worth more than pleasure, power, or vocational advancement.

He deemed faithfulness to God more valuable than even his own life. He gently freed himself from her grasp.

"I can't do this," he told her. "I can't sin against God."

"Don't mock me! Forget your god!" she cried. "I am offering myself to you!" She threw her arms around him again; they struggled, but he wrenched himself away. She grabbed at his coat and held on. "Sleep with me!" Her tone carried pleading, desperation, and threat.

Joseph slipped out of his coat and ran, leaving the garment in her hands. Behind him, he could hear her screaming with rage. The servants in the fields stopped their labors and stared wide-eyed at him as he flew out of the house door. Then her angry cries turned into a frenzy of vengeance.

"He tried to rape me! The Hebrew slave forced himself upon me then ran like the coward he is when I cried out!" She stood at the doorway of the house holding Joseph's cloak. "See! He left it in my hands when he fled!

"Seize him!"

A sickening dread came across Joseph. It was her word against his. There had been no other witnesses, except the One

A HARVEST OF FAITHFULNESS

to whom Joseph was faithful, the One who is called Faithful.

For Joseph, it was not a matter of being a faithful servant of Potiphar; being a faithful servant to God was far more important, even if it cost him his freedom and his life. But this was not the end for Joseph, but just the beginning. His faithful obedience to God put him on a path that eventually elevated him to a position that far superseded anything a slave could hope to accomplish.　　　　Based on GENESIS 39

Sowing In Tears, Reaping in Joy

As an editor of several women's special-interest magazines, Lou was in contact with a large and diverse group of writers, advertisers, and other publishers. She tried to use her influence to help them out whenever she could, believing that as a Christian, it was important to maintain good relationships with business associates, even competitors.

But when the CEO of the publishing company approached her about sharing an editorial with a new magazine being introduced by another publishing company, Lou balked.

"I didn't minded sharing my writers with a reputable publisher, but this was not a reputable publisher," said Lou.

While this publisher had a group of "legitimate" magazines, he also published a large number of pornographic titles promoting a whole range of other sexual perversions. Lou refused to introduce her writers to him.

"By introducing writers to him, I felt I was saying to them, 'I endorse this publishing company.' I emphatically could not. Even if I was not a born-again Christian, I could not have supported this man's sexual victimization of children and women. But by standing against his publishing company, my Christian faith became an issue, and it was used as a springboard for attack."

Lou mused that for those who don't understand how God upholds His children, bold identification with Christ is seen as a minus and a "chink in the armor."

"I turned the whole situation over to God. I felt that if I was fired for my stand against pornography and my identification with Christ was cited as the 'reason,' I would rejoice. I would rather work as a low-paid greeter in a department store and stand for Jesus than as a highly paid magazine editor who denied Christ. I needed to financially support my family, but we would do without if we had to and trust God to supply."

As the situation heated up and meetings between the CEO and Lou were charged with rancor toward her, Lou felt the stress.

"Every morning on the way to work, I would ask God to

178

be my Shield and Protector. I would pray for wisdom and a sweet spirit, because the CEO was trying to humiliate me publicly. I know that I have a tongue like a weed-whacker; I really wanted to shred that CEO!"

As quickly as the storm began, it was over. For a time, Lou didn't know what had happened, but the relationship between her company and the pornographer's had cooled. Later, by accident, she overheard the CEO telling another employee that the pornographer had "pulled a fast one" and that the publishing company was lucky to escape without further financial damage.

"Even if it hadn't come out favorable for me, standing with Christ was one of my proudest moments," said Lou. "Even if my career had come to an end, I would have had no regrets."

Faithful Example

Dear Father God,
Let me faithfully reflect what little of You I understand
to the world around me. Because I am crucified with
Christ, He lives in me. Whatever life I now live in my
flesh, I live by trusting the Son of God, who loved me and

gave Himself for me. You knew me before the foundations of the world. You predestined me to be conformed to the image of Your Son, so that He could be the first of Your many children. I am now Your child, and although I do not understand what I will become, I know that when Jesus appears, I shall be like Him, for I shall see Him as He is. I will behold Your face, and when I awake into eternity, it will be with Your likeness. In the meantime, let me be a faithful image of Your Son. Let my faith grow tall and strong, offering Your shelter to those around me.

Based on GALATIANS 2:20; ROMANS 8:29;
1 JOHN 3:2; PSALM 17:15

A HARVEST OF FAITHFULNESS

Dear Lord,
Let me be a willing and faithful servant of
Yours. As I have opportunity, help me to do good
unto all men.

Help me to love my neighbor as myself.
Help me to be merciful as You are merciful.
Help me not to judge lest I be judged.
Help me to be kind to others, tenderhearted,
*   and forgiving as You have forgiven me.*

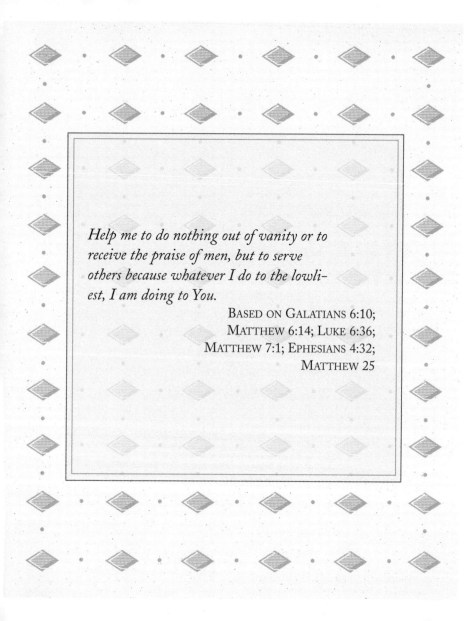

Help me to do nothing out of vanity or to receive the praise of men, but to serve others because whatever I do to the lowliest, I am doing to You.

BASED ON GALATIANS 6:10;
MATTHEW 6:14; LUKE 6:36;
MATTHEW 7:1; EPHESIANS 4:32;
MATTHEW 25

Chapter 8

Harvesting the Fruit of the Faith

And he shall be like a tree
planted by the rivers of water,
that bringeth forth
his fruit in his season;
his leaf also shall not wither;
and whatsoever he doeth
shall prosper.

PSALM 1:3

Faith is the seed; hope is the sprout; faithfulness is the fruit. Sometimes, it takes more than a lifetime for the fruit to ripen.

He that goeth forth and weepeth,

bearing precious seed,

shall doubtless come again

with rejoicing,

bringing his sheaves with him.

PSALM 126:6

Harvest in the Midst of Storms

While breast and liver cancer are literally eating Dawn alive, it took chemotherapy and radiation treatments to finally make her quit her job. "I've reached the point where I have to go on disability," Dawn says, readjusting her turban to cover her baldness. "Before I had this job, I lived hand-to-mouth, so I know

God provides. But once I had this job, I committed myself financially to supporting some mission projects. I knew my disability check would be so much less than what I had been earning. So I prayed, 'Lord, what am I going to do about my mission projects? I don't want to give less.' "

As Dawn was cleaning out her desk on her final day of work, she was handed a bonus envelope containing $100. Thankful, she tucked it in her purse to take to the bank. On her way out of the building, a coworker stopped her with news. A mutual friend's husband had just had open-heart surgery, she said, and their family was in terrible financial straits. The government programs had not yet kicked in, the husband needed medicine, and the family had exhausted all their reserves.

As Dawn listened, she prayed, *Lord, I wish I could help.* She felt as though the Lord nudged her. *You've got $100 in your purse!*

As Dawn handed her coworker the envelope she had just received, she felt the Lord's assurance that as long as she lived by faith, God would provide for both her needs and the commitments she had made to His work.

"I don't know how He's going to do it, but it will be an adventure to watch Him work." She smiles, not a trace of fear on her face. "Maybe this will be my final adventure in faith."

The righteous
will live by faith.

ROMANS 1:17 NIV

Reaping Faith's Harvest
Faithfulness to God in Life's Most Trying Moments

Our pain is enormous. Every encouraging word seems trite. The heavens appear to made of brass. God's throne is out of reach. Where is God?

These are the moments that try our faith. Can we still faithfully believe that God loves us when He is allowing such pain? Can we still faithfully believe in His justice when the wicked are prospering and we are not?

But, in truth, these are the moments when we reap the rich harvest of faithfulness!

Fruit by Choice

We cannot bear fruit by merely making up our minds and then trying very hard to do so, any more than a grapevine can grow grapes because it wishes to.

Like the grapevine, we will naturally produce fruit if we attach ourselves to the Vine and open wide our veins to the work of the Spirit. Then watch the fruit grow!

No coward soul is mine,
No trembler in the world's storm-troubled sphere:
I see Heaven's glories shine,
And faith shines equal, arming me from fear.
EMILY BRONTË

The Sweet Fruit of a Faithful Relationship with God

Our faith in God is lived out in our faithfulness to Him; faith and action are the legs that support our walk with Him. The more we trust God to be faithful to us, the more we will be willing to step out to do His will—and the farther and faster we will move His kingdom forward on earth.

Harvesting Faithfulness with Tears of Hope
The Rainbow's Promise of Faithfulness

One day last summer, Linda called me to invite me to a birthday party for Jody, our pastor's wife. I was delighted to accept.

At the party, we laughed and shared stories. Since both Jody and Linda cried at the drop of a hat, Linda had a special birthday gift for her: a cut crystal bowl converted into a tissue holder. She held up the crystal bowl to catch a beam of summer sunshine. It threw rainbows around the room, decorating all of us with patches of brilliance.

"I love crystal," Linda began, "not just because it's beautiful, but it reminds me of the beauty Jesus makes with common people."

Linda related how crystal was formed by heating common sand to great temperatures. Then the glass was faceted by a master glass cutter to give it sparkle, dimension, and individual characteristics.

"This is our lives in Jesus," said Linda, rotating the bowl to make the rainbows dance, dazzling our eyes. "He allows trials to heat us, because He wants to transform the sand in our souls to crystal. He lets sorrow cut us so we have more surfaces where the Son can shine through us and show the world rainbows."

Then Linda talked about Noah and the Great Flood and how God sent a rainbow as a promise of His faithfulness. "I keep tissues in my crystal bowl so that each time I reach for one to wipe away a flood of tears, I know God is only making me more beautiful, more reflective of Him. I know that after my flood of tears, God will make rainbows of my sorrow."

We sat in silence, regarding the bowl and its glistening colors. We all knew that Linda was speaking from her own adventures in faith. In her lifetime, she had experienced many cuts on her crystal surfaces, but Jesus was reflected through each of them.

I noticed that day how tired Linda looked. Although she was only in her midfifties, she was fighting assorted health problems, but her major worry was for her husband Mike, who was struggling with a potentially deadly heart condition.

"Pray that Mike lives long enough to see our son married," she had begged me earlier in the summer.

By the time of the surprise birthday, their son's wedding

had come and gone, and now Mike was doing great. Her prayers and mine had been answered. *Now she can rest a little,* I thought. As the party broke up, I kissed Linda on the cheek and left.

The next evening, my phone rang with startling news: Linda was dead. She had died in her sleep from an unsuspected heart condition.

Several days later, as a violent, late-afternoon thunderstorm rocked the city, I stood in line at the funeral home to view Linda's body. As the line slowly wound by the open coffin, the storm abated and the sun shone wanly, as if uncertain whether to attempt to dry things off or just set for the night.

When I reached Linda's coffin, I stopped still. Across the bridge of her nose a little rainbow shone. Puzzled, I looked around for a prism, something that would explain the errant light, but I never found an answer. Then I remembered Linda's words the day of the party. After this life's showers of tears comes heavenly beauty. Linda's entire life had been a rainbow, a faithful witness to God, who keeps His promises.

Are you debating whether you should take a step of faith in Jesus, or whether you should wait until you can clearly see how to do what He has asked? Simply obey Him with unrestrained joy. When He tells you something and you begin to debate, it is because you have a misunderstanding of what honors Him and what doesn't. Are you faithful to Jesus, or faithful to your ideas about Him? Are you faithful to what He says, or are you trying to compromise His words with thoughts that never came from Him? "Whatever He says to you, do it" (John 2:5 NKJV).

OSWALD CHAMBERS
My Utmost for His Highest

Faithfulness in Prayer

Watching your parents get old is like an old childhood nightmare—the one where you dream your parents have abandoned you, leaving you alone to face the world. I'm glad that no matter how old my parents get, I know I will always be supported by their faithful love and prayer.

My dad is now approaching ninety, but despite his various aches and pains, he is still amazingly healthy and in good shape.

Still, he gets frustrated that he is no longer able to roof the house, hop in and out of the car with ease, and carry eighty pounds of whatever as though it were nothing. But still true to his calling as pastor, he and Mother visit the old folks at the nursing home, many of whom are much younger than both of them. But getting around is harder for him. Icy ground is a hazard. Darkness is a barrier. So now what? It must be hard to go from being 6-foot-4-inches with a brace of shoulders as strong as a crowbar to spending the day in his recliner because his knees hurt and he feels weak. Inside, he still wants to serve.

So he does. From his recliner, he has a ministry of prayer.

If he knows that any of his large family (nearly seventy souls at this writing) has anything happening—a road trip, a test, an illness, a challenge—he is on the phone to pray with them, Mother on the extension agreeing in prayer. Whenever I face a crisis in my life, I am empowered by this knowledge: Dad and Mother are praying. God has been alerted, and His throne is under siege on my behalf. I can walk in faith.

Sometimes Dad writes down his prayers for his children and grandchildren. In my wallet, I carry one of his prayers, creased and folded. He wrote it at a time when my family and I were in great need, a time when we needed a divine act to resolve the situation. During those troubled times, when I was surrounded by overwhelming troubles, each time I reread Dad's prayer, I could hear the thunderous hoofbeats of the hosts of heaven riding to my rescue.

The prayer is a simple one, seven brief sentences, including the salutation to my father's Heavenly Father. He begins his prayer claiming a promise of God on our behalf and ends with a note of thanks. Written in his own hand on plain white paper, it has been burned into my heart. I know that it is also inscribed in gold in the *Lamb's Book of Life*.

I have faith in thee, O my God, that Thou wilt not leave me, that Thou wilt not permit me to go astray; but wilt keep me in all inward thought, as well as in all outward word and action. CATHERINE OF GENOA

Down in adoration falling, Lo!
The sacred host we hail;
. . . Faith for all defects supplying,
where the feeble senses fail.

THOMAS AQUINAS

Faith is the soul's consciousness of its divine relationship and exalted destiny. It is the recognition by man's higher nature of sources of comfort and hope beyond anything that sense-knowledge discloses. It is the consciousness of a divine Father toward whom goes out all that is in affection and highest in moral aspiration; it is the premonition of a future life of which the best attainment here is but the twilight promise. In our day, the sudden and vast revelation of material wonders unsteadies and dims for the moment the spiritual sight; but the stars will shine clear again. The truth-seeking spirit and the spirit of faith, instead of being opposed, are in the deepest harmony. The man whose faith is most genuine is most willing to have its assertions tested by the severest scrutiny. And the passion for truth has underlying it a profound conviction that what is real is best; that when we get to the heart of things we shall find there what we most need. Faith is false to itself when it dreads truth, and the desire for truth is prompted by an inner voice of faith.

GEORGE SPRINGS MIRRIAM

A Living Faith

Our hearts, our hopes,

our prayers, our tears,

our faith triumphant o'er

our fears,

are all with thee—

are all with thee!

HENRY WADSWORTH LONGFELLOW

Faithfully Yielding Fruit Among the Boulders of Oppression
Adoniram Judson

The Burmese were at war with the British, and all they could see when they looked at missionary Adoniram Judson was that he was an Anglo. It made no difference to them that he was an American who had been preaching and teaching in their country for nine years, nor that it was the British, not the Americans, with whom they were at war. Judson must be a spy, they concluded, and so they imprisoned him.

While there is never a convenient time to be imprisoned, this was particularly bad timing for Adoniram. He had labored six years in Burma before the first person came to Christ, but the last few years had proved fruitful to the kingdom. Adoniram had finished his translation of a Burmese New Testament, converts were coming to the Lord, and he had won the approval of the king of Burma. His wife Ann was expecting a child, recovering from her grief over the one that had been stillborn during their initial voyage to Burma. But this time of blessing was only the calm before the storm, for 1824 not only saw escalating hostilities between Britain and Burma, but now Adoniram had been arrested and imprisoned. Thrown into one of Burma's infamous vermin-infested "death" prisons with common criminals, Adoniram endured nightly torture. His ankles were bound together and secured to a suspended pole, so that only his head and shoulders touched the cold earth. By day, he was tightly confined in the packed prison, unable to stretch his cramped, sore muscles. Brave Ann bribed the brutal guards so she could smuggle in food. During the time when their child was born, however, Adoniram was transferred to another prison without Ann's knowledge. No one would tell her where he went or whether he was dead or alive.

A HARVEST OF FAITHFULNESS

Adoniram wasn't entirely sure himself. Already emaciated and frail, he and the other prisoners were marched barefoot in the merciless heat over gravel roads to another prison. Here he languished for a year and half until he was released from prison to be an interpreter for the peace negotiations.

He had a joyous but brief reunion with Ann and the baby. Then he was summoned to the negotiations. While he was away, both Ann and the baby perished.

Most men would have given up at that point and returned to the States with its relative comfort and safety, but Adoniram believed he had been called by God to serve in Burma. He plunged himself back into his translating work. But his imprisonment, torture, and grief exacted their toll; he fell into a disabling depression.

For forty days, great despondency paralyzed him; but through the prayers and encouragement of other missionaries, he eventually was able to shake off the despondency and continue his ministry. Rather than being broken by his experiences, they only served to make him into a more useable tool for the kingdom.

Wrote Adoniram concerning the revival that swept Burma: "I sometimes feel alarmed, like a person who sees a mighty engine beginning to move, over which he knows he has not control."

In the years that followed, Judson faithfully completed his

translation of the Old Testament, and the Burmese church grew mightily. It continues to grow to this day under difficult circumstances. The fruit of Adoniram Judson's faithfulness still nourishes our world.

Wherefore seeing we also are compassed about with so great a cloud of witnesses, let us lay aside every weight, and the sin which doth so easily beset us, and let us run with patience the race that is set before us, looking unto Jesus the author and finisher of our faith; who for the joy that was set before him endured the cross, despising the shame, and is set down at the right hand of the throne of God. HEBREWS 12:1–2

'Tis not the dying for a faith that's so hard. . .' 'tis the living up to it that's difficult.

WILLIAM MAKEPEACE THACKERAY

A HARVEST OF FAITHFULNESS

A Rich Harvest
From the Bread of Life, with Love

It was one of those weeks in Beth's household. Although her husband made a good living, occasionally between paychecks the checkbook was a little flat. This was one of those times.

With growing children, food was always needed. Beth was running low on some staple items, but in light of the bank balance, she decided to keep her purchases to a minimum. As she walked the grocery aisles contemplating her family's needs, she saw the baking supplies and bags of flour.

Oh, yes, thought Beth, *I need flour. And when you need flour, you need flour. It's not like God drops flour off on the doorstep!*

She picked up a five-pound bag and purchased it.

Back home, as she put away the groceries, her doorbell rang. There stood her neighbor's son. He handed a round tin to Beth.

"Mom said to give you this."

Beth knew her neighbors were Jewish folks who had decided to go kosher, but what she found inside the tin made her laugh out loud at God's sense of humor.

It was a five-pound bag of flour.

Christian faith is, then, not only an assent to the whole gospel of Christ, but also a full reliance on the blood of Christ; a trust in the merits of His life, death, and resurrection; a recumbency on Him as our atonement and our life, as given for us, and living in us.   JOHN WESLEY

Tearing Down the Walls Between Us and the Harvest of Faith

Remember Joshua and the wall of Jericho? The wall around the city seemed insurmountable—but through faith, all things are possible. Even the strongest, tallest walls come tumbling down when faith blows its horn. And then you will see the richest fruits of faith waiting to be picked.

If you are facing a wall, you too can surmount it if you don't give up but remain obedient to the end.

I will call upon the LORD, who is worthy to be
praised: so shall I be saved from mine enemies.

PSALM 18:3

◆ Therefore: If you call upon the Lord, your enemies will fall down.

The LORD is my strength and my shield;
my heart trusted in him, and I am helped.

PSALM 28:7

◆ Therefore: If you trust in God, the walls of helplessness will fall down.

Being justified by faith, we have peace with God
through our Lord Jesus Christ.   ROMANS 5:1

◆ Therefore: If you have faith in God, the walls of conflict will fall down.

If any of you lacks wisdom, he should ask God,
who gives generously to all without finding fault,
and it will be given to him.   JAMES 1:5

◆ Therefore: If you ask God for wisdom, the walls of uncertainty will fall down.

Believe on the Lord Jesus Christ, and thou shalt be saved, and thy house. ACTS 16:31

◆ Therefore: If you believe on the Lord Jesus Christ, the walls of hell will fall down.

Blessed is the man that endureth temptation: for when he is tried, he shall receive the crown of life, which the Lord hath promised to them that love him. JAMES 1:3

◆ Therefore: If you endure temptation, the throne room of Life will open up to you.

The Shout of Faith

And it came to pass, when. . .the people shouted with a great shout, that the wall fell flat.

JOSHUA 6:20

A HARVEST OF FAITHFULNESS

The walls may look as high and immovable as ever; and prudence may say it is not safe to shout until the victory is actually won. But the faith that can shout in the midst of the sorest stress of temptation, "Jesus saves me; He saves me now!" such a faith will be sure to win a glorious and speedy victory. Many of God's children have tried this plan, and have found it to work far beyond their expectations. Temptations have come upon them like a flood; temptations to irritability, or to wicked thoughts, or to bitterness of spirit, or to a thousand other things, and they have seen their danger; and their fears and their feelings have declared there was no hope of escape. But their faith has laid hold of the grand fact that Christ has conquered; and they have fixed their gaze on the unseen power of God's salvation, and have given their shout of victory. "The Lord saves! He saves me now! I am more than conqueror through Him that loves me!" And the result is always a glorious victory.

HANNAH WHITALL SMITH

When God Transforms
the Wall into a Way

When Bill told his wife he felt called to go to Russia as a missionary, she pointed out a problem. "You're terrible at learning languages!"

How could he master Russian? Recalling a miracle in Acts where all the listeners heard the gospel in their own language (Acts 2:8–12), Bill told her, "Maybe God will give me a gift so I can speak and understand Russian."

Shortly after their arrival in Russia, however, Bill soon realized that fluent Russian was not going to pour off his tongue. Even purchasing groceries challenged his linguistic prowess. "I thought I ordered hamburger but I accidentally bought dog food—which became apparent as soon as we started frying it!" said Bill.

But Bill claimed God's promise in John 15:5 (NIV): "If a man remains in me and I in him, he will bear much fruit."

For a year and a half, Bill taught a Bible-based curriculum through interpreters. The interpreters' quest for answers to the students' questions sent them searching the Bible and many came to faith in Christ. Bill's dependence upon interpreters was yielding unsuspected fruit. As they struggled to translate doctrine, they too studied the Scriptures.

"As the Holy Spirit worked through these non-Christian

interpreters, they came to faith in Christ," said Bill. "This just blew away what the mission organization's philosophy was on learning the language of the people." Bill grinned. "When you're a missionary to a foreign country, you should always learn the language—unless God decides to do something different!"

Faithfully Harvesting Faith During a Cold Season
Feet Like a Deer's

Tom and Chris were eagerly anticipating the birth of a grandchild when their joy was cut short by frightening news. "At a routine seven-month check, the doctor told our daughter Cindy that the baby had water on the brain. He sent her to an obstetrical specialist," said Chris.

The second diagnosis confirmed the first: The baby had hydrocephalus. It also revealed the crippling condition of spina bifida.

"The best you can hope," the second doctor said, "is that your child will be wheelchair-bound but not mentally incapacitated."

However, before Cindy and her husband left the specialist's

office, she already trusted God was at work. "I know God has a special purpose for this baby. He will use this child to reach people," Cindy said.

The entire family was devastated by the baby's many problems. Some even argued for an abortion. The baby's grandparents, Chris and Tom, searched for answers. "God showed me Habakkuk 3:16–19 in the *New International Version*," Chris said.

This Scripture passage deals with a time when God's beloved people are hearing rumors of trouble on all sides, and yet —"I heard and my heart pounded, my lips quivered. . .and my legs trembled. . .(but) though the fig tree does not bud, and there are no grapes on the vines, though the olive crop fails and the fields produce no food, though there are no sheep in the pen and no cattle in the stalls, yet I will rejoice in the LORD, I will be joyful in God my Savior. The Sovereign LORD is my strength; he makes my feet like the feet of a deer, he enables me to go on the heights."

"I told our daughter, 'You could substitute our names in this passage. The words fit us.' "

Zachary was born a short time later with all of the promised challenges. While he is still very young, he does not appear to be mentally incapacitated.

"He rolled over at five months," said Chris. "He is the happiest, cutest, most adorable baby ever. We don't know what's

A HARVEST OF FAITHFULNESS

ahead, but God has promised He will walk with us over our mountains."

With the hooves of the surefooted deer.

It is only a faithful person who truly believes that God sovereignly controls his circumstances. We take our circumstances for granted, saying God is in control, but not really believing it. We act as if the things that happen were completely controlled by people. To be faithful in every circumstance means that we have only one loyalty, or object of our faith—the Lord Jesus Christ. God may cause our circumstances to suddenly fall apart, which may bring the realization of our unfaithfulness to Him for not recognizing that He had ordained the situation. We never saw what He was trying to accomplish, and that exact event will never be repeated in our life. This is where the test of our faithfulness comes. If we will just learn to worship God even during the difficult circumstances, He will change them for the better very quickly if He so chooses. OSWALD CHAMBERS

An Invitation to a Feast

While the fruit of the Tree of the Knowledge of Good and Evil brought death, partaking of the fruit of the Spirit brings life-abundant, fulfilling, powerful! Jesus demonstrated this with His very life.

We know from witnessing the life cycle of the fruit of the Spirit that faithfulness requires surrender to the Holy Spirit. Without the sap of the Holy Spirit flowing into our hearts and minds, we produce a diseased, stunted variety of faithfulness that is in no way healthy or wholesome to us or the people around us.

The Holy Spirit doesn't force Himself down anyone's throat. In a still, small voice, He invites us to dine at the Lord's table. When His life-giving Spirit flows within us, seeds of faithfulness are planted with us. In no time, we are nourished, fulfilled, blooming, and fruit-bearing!

With our cooperation, the Holy Spirit begins to plant, prune, and train our souls, then faithfulness grows luxuriantly with absolutely miraculous results in our relationships!

Come and dine at the table of spiritual fruit.

Taste and see that

the LORD is good!

PSALM 34:8

The ABC's of Faithfulness

A *A faithful man shall abound with blessings.*

PROVERBS 28:20

B *Be thou faithful unto death, and I will give thee a crown of life.*

REVELATION 2:10

C *Continue thou in the things which thou hast learned and hast been assured of, knowing of whom thou hast learned them.*

2 TIMOTHY 3:14

D *Deliver my soul: oh save me for thy mercies' sake.*

PSALM 6:4

E   *I will make an Everlasting covenant with them, that I will not turn away from them, to do them good; but I will put my fear in their hearts, that they shall not depart from me.*

JEREMIAH 32:40

F   *For I am persuaded, that neither death, nor life, nor angels, nor principalities, nor powers, nor things present, nor things to come, nor height, nor depth, nor any other creature, shall be able to separate us from the love of God, which is in Jesus Christ our Lord.*

ROMANS 8:38–39

G   *God is with thee in all that thou doest.*   GENESIS 21:22

H   *Hold fast the form of sound words, which thou hast heard of me, in faith and love which is in Christ Jesus.*

2 TIMOTHY 1:13

J   *I know whom I have believed, and am persuaded that he is able to keep that which I have committed unto him against that day.*   2 TIMOTHY 1:12

J   *Then said Jesus to those Jews which believed on him, "If you continue in my word, then are ye my disciples indeed."*

JOHN 8:31

A HARVEST OF FAITHFULNESS

K   *Keep mercy and judgment, and wait on thy God continually.*   HOSEA 12:6

L   *Let us hold fast the profession of our faith without wavering; (for he is faithful that promised).*   HEBREWS 10:23

M   *My heart is fixed; I will sing and give praise.*   PSALM 108:1

N   *Now no chastening for the present seemeth to be joyous, but grievous: nevertheless afterwards it yieldeth the peaceable fruit of righteousness unto them which are exercised thereby.*   HEBREW 12:11

O   *O love the LORD, all ye his saints: for the LORD preserveth the faithful.*   PSALM 31:23

P   *Prove all things; hold fast that which is good.*   1 THESSALONIANS 5:21

Q   *It is good that a man should both hope and Quietly wait for the salvation of the LORD.*   LAMENTATIONS 3:26

R   *Rooted and built up in him, and stablished in the faith.*   COLOSSIANS 2:7

S   *Stand fast in the Lord.*   PHILIPPIANS 4:1

T   *Take, my brethren, the prophets, who have spoken in the name of the Lord, for an example of suffering affliction, and of patience.*

JAMES 5:10

U   *Though he fall, he shall not be Utterly cast down: for the* LORD *upholdeth him with his hand.*

PSALM 37:24

V   *Be Vigilant: because your adversary the devil, as a roaring lion, walketh about, seeking whom he may devour.*

1 PETER 5:8

W   *Watch ye, stand fast in the faith, quit you like men, be strong.*

1 CORINTHIANS 16:13

Y   *Ye are washed. . .ye are sanctified, . . .ye are justified in the name of the Lord Jesus, and by the Spirit of our God.*

1 CORINTHIANS 6:11

Z   *Ye are come unto mount [Z]ion, and unto the city of the living God, the heavenly Jerusalem, and to an innumerable company of angels.*

HEBREWS 12:22

A HARVEST OF FAITHFULNESS

A Through Z

The Bible says that Jesus is the Alpha and the Omega. Translated into our alphabet, this means He is the "A" and the "Z"—the beginning and the end. He is the source of the seeds of faith planted in our hearts; He is the One who will help those seeds put down deep roots and grow to maturity; and He is the One who will bring our faith to completion, so that He can harvest the fruits of faithfulness from our lives.

Looking unto Jesus
the author and finisher
of our faith. . .

HEBREWS 12:2

This vine did bend her
roots toward him,
and shot forth her
branches toward him,
that he might water it. . . .
It was planted in a good soil
by great waters,
that it might bring forth branches,
and that it might bear fruit,
that it might be a goodly vine.

 EZEKIEL 17:7–8

A HARVEST OF FAITHFULNESS

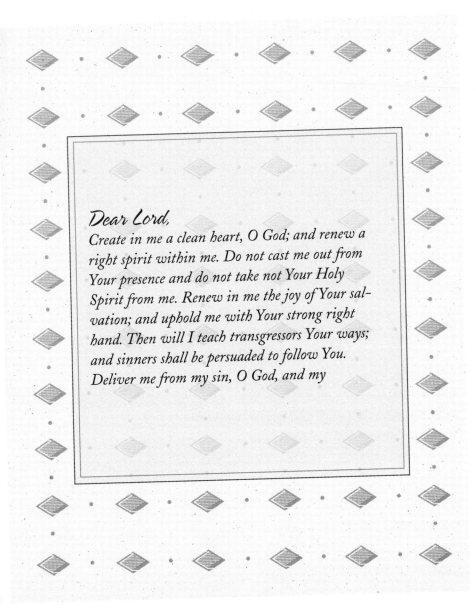

Dear Lord,
Create in me a clean heart, O God; and renew a
right spirit within me. Do not cast me out from
Your presence and do not take not Your Holy
Spirit from me. Renew in me the joy of Your sal-
vation; and uphold me with Your strong right
hand. Then will I teach transgressors Your ways;
and sinners shall be persuaded to follow You.
Deliver me from my sin, O God, and my

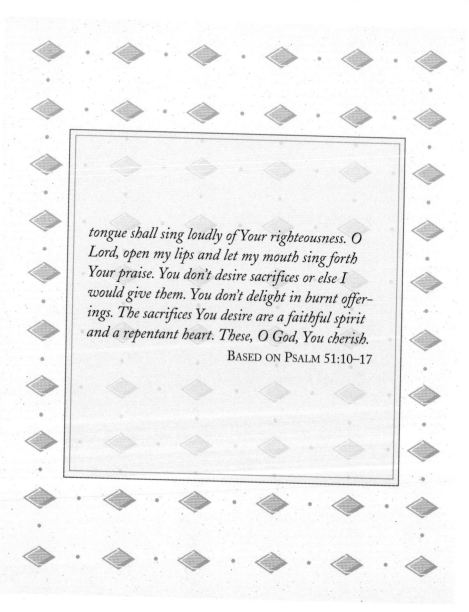

tongue shall sing loudly of Your righteousness. O Lord, open my lips and let my mouth sing forth Your praise. You don't desire sacrifices or else I would give them. You don't delight in burnt offerings. The sacrifices You desire are a faithful spirit and a repentant heart. These, O God, You cherish.

BASED ON PSALM 51:10–17

About the Author

Rebekah Montgomery has over thirty years of experience as a pastor and teacher. A prolific writer, she is the author of several books; many magazine, newspaper, and inspirational articles; camp and Bible school curriculum; and children's musicals. Rebekah is the author of *Ordinary Miracles: True Stories of an Extraordinary God Who Works in Our Everyday Lives* (Promise Press, May 2000), and is presently developing a book series on the *Fruit of the Spirit* (Promise Press, July 2000).

Rebekah lives in Kewanee, Illinois, with John, her husband of thirty years, and their three children, Mary, Joel, and Daniel.

Look for other books in this series...

A HARVEST OF JOY • A HARVEST OF Love

A HARVEST OF Faithfulness

A HARVEST OF Peace

$8.99 each • 224 pages

Available wherever books are sold.

Or order from:
Barbour Publishing
P.O. Box 719
Uhrichsville, Ohio 44683
www.barbourbooks.com

If you order by mail, add $2.00 to your order for shipping.
Prices subject to change without notice.